UNPLEASANTRIES

FRANK SOOS

Unpleasantries

CONSIDERATIONS *of*
DIFFICULT QUESTIONS

UNIVERSITY OF WASHINGTON PRESS
Seattle and London

UNIVERSITY OF WASHINGTON PRESS
www.washington.edu/uwpress

LIBRARY OF CONGRESS CATALOGING-IN-PUBLICATION DATA
Names: Soos, Frank, author.
Title: Unpleasantries : considerations of difficult questions / Frank Soos.
Description: Seattle : University of Washington Press, 2016.
Identifiers: LCCN 2015048156 | ISBN 9780295998404 (hardcover : alk. paper)
Classification: LCC PS3569.O663 A6 2016 | DDC 814/.54—dc23
LC record available at http://lccn.loc.gov/2015048156

For Margot

With love and gratitude

CONTENTS

PREFACE

I'm a messy guy. My desk is a mess covered by sliding piles of paper, my workbench is a mess so the tool I need is rarely at hand, my personal library is a mess with books shelved in no reliable order and stacked all over the floor. The essay can be a messy form; maybe that's why I write them.

Still, a person should try to be neat. Fiction can be neat. Writing a good short story is typically about diminishing choices. Each juncture of a plot is a reduction of characters' options. I like to write short stories. I like that process of funneling down until I can find that final action, the only satisfactory action.

Life isn't much like fiction, though. When my cousin Lou fell off a ladder while at work, this method of finding meaning through putting characters into action would not do. Lou was dead, dead on the day he signed the mortgage for his new house, dead leaving a widow and two small sons to grow up without him.

That news arrived as no kind of story with its attendant rising action and complications, and no story I might invent could make sense of Lou's death. Once there was a man, now there was a void. With no larger purpose than to try to fill that void I felt in my heart, I began making notes to myself. Blurts, I've come to call them. And those blurts seemed to pop up anywhere, in the back of a composition class I was observing, as I drove to and from school, when I unfolded the schematic diagram in the back of my motorcycle owner's manual, when I went home to see my family. Here was a dilemma that would not let go of me.

As I wrote down these notes, as I struggled to come to an understanding, I began by accident to build what became an essay. What other form could hold this kind of information?

How any one of my blurts might lead to another is a bafflement to me. But I think my brain and your brain, reader, work this way. Our thoughts are not linear, and when we begin thinking of X and then discover we're thinking of Y instead and can't remember the chain of thoughts that took us from X to Y, we have demonstrated in a small way the path an essay may often take. Our thought processes are not unlike those wonderful pinball machines found in every café, truck stop, and beer joint when I was a kid. Put the ball in play, keep it going with the flippers, and pretty soon all the bumpers are lit and the ball is jumping back and forth between them. Each bumper could be an idea, an emotion, a metaphor, a little anecdote, all linked by that silver ball.

The act of lighting those brain bumpers is much slower than the nearly instantaneous actions of a pinball machine. Just as beyond our full control, though. The electric impulses in my brain shoot ideas around as if they have a life of their own. Blurts happen. I write slowly, build a big body of blurts until I see I must cut much of what I've written.

That's the hard part. If I may switch metaphors and mix them as well: the narrowing down that makes fiction (still difficult but) manageable doesn't happen in the essay. Rather, it's the opposite. Every idea generates multitudes of follow-on ideas. Instead of the tidy combination that gets the eight ball in the side pocket, the combinations simply keep multiplying, a huge chain reaction of thought, an unmanageable slide of ideas that in some way are all linked—if only because they came out of one single head.

At such a point, I've hardly made any effort to give an essay a form. At such a point, I'm simply looking for some linkages among my many blurts that might begin to show me which ones will be part of the essay, which are contributing to my question. Which are leaning toward some central gravitational pull and which are leaning away? This process is not about rational thought, but about feel, about intuition.

I should admit that the essay is a way of getting at questions I can't get at by any other means. And I should also admit that I often don't know how to frame the question I may be chasing or where my chase will lead. Essays of this type can be confusing. They rarely proceed in a linear fashion; they are often inconclusive. The abrupt transitions between segments open chasms where readers might fall in and become lost among my thoughts or among their own.

The questions I care most about don't have easy answers. These are questions of how we live with one another, how we live with other animals, how to make meaning of this life, how to value it aesthetically. In fact, such questions may have no answers at all. Still, they must be asked.

In writing this way, I am not simply writing for my own hopes of self-discovery (when Montaigne makes this claim for his essays, he's plainly indulging in a little ironic joke). I am writing for a reader who might somehow be on the same scent. So I've tried to retain the lurching style employed in my search in hopes that the reader will be tempted to try some similar sideways questioning and see if he or she doesn't find new ways of thinking that never occurred to me. My aim is often to put an idea in play and keep it in play, but not bring it fully to rest. To keep the idea going beyond the close of an essay is always my hope.

And I hope readers will think along with me, will stop from time to time and carry forward with ideas of their own. The questions matter more than any possible answer.

Recently I was offered an invitation to talk to a group of writers about any aspect of the essay I chose. I thought, *What a good place to start*, because of all the reasons the essay has appealed to me, its open-ended structure might be at the top of the list. In a recent workshop, I wrote across the top of the white board what I hoped would be our class motto: "You can't do this wrong; but you can do it better." Right. You can't do it wrong.

Every essay rolls out in its own way, finding its own narrow path as it goes.

I find I must depend on the goodwill of my readers. A welcoming tone helps. But what matters most is that the questions of my life somehow speak to the questions others might have. Maybe I should say "must have," because I believe my questions are all of our questions. How can a person live fully in the world without examining his place in it? The essay is as good a place as any to start.

UNPLEASANTRIES

Another Kind of Loneliness

It is dark outside. I'm alone in the ski hut, adding layer on layer to my ski clothes. Though some few trails at the university in Fairbanks are lighted, I will take the longer, darker path through the woods. The last thing I do is strap on my headlamp, feeding the battery pack down my back under all my clothes so it will stay warm next to my skin.

This may be crazy, setting out alone when it is already twenty below. But I know these trails so well that when I cannot sleep, one of my tricks to overcome insomnia is to ski them in my mind. Each hill, each turn, I travel behind the science buildings, the student apartments and married student housing, across the small lake, and then seemingly deeper into the woods on the other side, because I am never really that far from a road. It's there that I have sometimes met the great horned owl, heard it first and then spotted it. Once it spat down one of its compacted regurgitated pellets, sending it tumbling into the snow at the base of the big spruce where it roosted. A gift? A judgment?

In America it is almost a criminal offense to be lonely. At the very least it's unhealthy. Crazy, as I've said. Roy Orbison (bleating): "Only the lonely know the way I feel tonight / Only the lonely know this feeling ain't right . . ."

I need to be here alone in these woods.

For thirty years I made my living as a teacher, a reluctant public man. Teaching has its many pleasures. It also has its costs for a shy person. Somehow I knew I could teach in the way that equally shy people know they can go onstage and act. The two are not un-

3

related. Up there in front of a class, I was a performer with a clear role. Up there, I spent a good bit of energy keeping myself inflated. Students have a right to expect you to be pretty much the same person every day. I could do that; it was something I was good at. But to do it, I had to go away from people to get my self back.

I am a most mooselike man, tall, gangly, clumsy, and slow, above all an animal given to loneliness. Moose, except for those moments when the urge to mate comes over them, would rather be alone. You might see them in any weather, nosing in the snow browsing for willow shoots, standing in lakes reaching to the bottom for weeds. You will rarely see them, male moose particularly, in the company of other moose. Moose are ruminants.

My wife Margot's son has recently returned from Africa, from Ethiopia and Namibia. He went to India as a junior in college and has returned there many times. I have no interest in these places. Rightly or wrongly, in my mind they stand for crowds of people. Here are places I imagine myself going to: the high desert of the American Southwest, the Arctic National Wildlife Refuge, the open ocean. Having been to the refuge once, I would go again, stay longer in a place where sometimes a person can go for hours without hearing another human-generated sound, that of a passing airplane.

Having tried once unsuccessfully to take part in a Quaker meeting, I know I am no good at what the Buddhists call sitting. I cannot be still, cannot quiet my mind. Though I tried a time or two, I see now I have no interest in quieting my mind. That people can and do amazes and baffles me.

I am a ruminant, too.

Once on my skis, I step into the set tracks and begin. At first I am inclined to move too fast, to rush through the glide that makes skiing skiing, not just running on boards. When I come to the first long flat, I double-pole, driving myself along by planting and pushing off both poles simultaneously, and then add a one-legged kick to the motion, a kick-double-pole. Finally, I return to a stride and begin to find a rhythm I can relax into. I seem to myself to be going more slowly, but actually I am moving faster than the herky-jerky way I began.

Rather than a skier, I was made to be a basketball player. In my fashion I was one. I could run the floor, jump high, block shots and rebound, even shoot a little on some nights. Basketball, though, is a social game, as socially complicated as any game I know. Each player is endowed, at least in principle, with all the same powers, to go anywhere on the court, to pass, to shoot from anywhere. Each player must share these powers with his teammates in complex proportions in accordance with his skills. The only hierarchy on a basketball floor is one imposed by the players themselves and their coach. Here is where I got into trouble. With every missed shot, every bad pass, I imagined my teammates passing judgment on me, and deservedly so. Some games, I got so I wouldn't shoot the ball at all. Who was I to be taking another shot when I had just missed one two feet from the basket?

Every Sunday in season I ski with a group of guys, the SCUM, Sugai's Class of Uncoachable Men. Incrementally, Susan Sugai, our volunteer coach, chemical oceanographer by training and university administrator by profession, has made us better skiers. Along the way SCUM has become a social institution as well. The old ski hut in Fairbanks' Birch Hill Recreation Area has become our de facto clubhouse. Sometimes we come together to clear trails, have a season-ending potluck, go on summer bike rides. These are good people, good friends. We kid around; we sometimes work out pretty hard; nobody blames me for skiing poorly or envies me in the unlikely event I ski well. But SCUM probably stretches me to the limit of my sociability. In the jostling give-and-take, I find myself yearning to hit the trail, to ski away to quietude.

In that quiet, what do I do? What do I think about out there, my headlamp bobbing along in the dark? What should I do beyond putting one ski ahead of the other? Sometimes, I am ashamed to say, I review perceived slights and recriminations, fresh quarrels: things somebody said or did that seemed hurtful to me somehow. I grind away at such an event over and over, review every detail of what was said and what I might have said or done in response. I grind it to dust, wear it out. Eventually I just can't mess with it anymore. Somehow the hurt is made to go away. Is this what the psychologists mean by "working through" a problem?

If I truly am like a moose, it seems like I should have a tougher hide.

Maybe instead I should seek to know myself better. Samuel Beckett believed we could never come to know ourselves fully, no matter how hard we tried. I think I believe that as well, but I think, perhaps like Beckett himself, a person still has to keep seeking to know. But where? And how?

I could do like Montaigne and ceaselessly fork over every thought that goes through my head. Montaigne compared his own restless mind to "masses and shapeless lumps of flesh" or to a field left fallow and allowed to go to weeds. In other words, a mess-making machine.

What's up there in my head is like a big balloon. Skiing along, I fill the balloon with words, images, things seen, things heard, things imagined. Many of these thoughts must be so private they can be shared with nobody else. Not because they are banal, sexual, or self-aggrandizing and therefore embarrassing, morally questionable, or possibly crazy if exposed to the light of day, but because they are just so many shapeless lumps. Taken together, they make a landscape that exists in my head and my head only. In this way they are like the paintings of Yves Tanguy. What are some of those strange tuberous things? Those figures that could belong on cave walls, in kindergarten drawings, in art-as-therapy? Those shapes that look like jigsaw puzzle pieces, parsnips, amoebas, architecture from another planet? It would be wrong to call them misshapen, because they rarely attempt to represent anything we know. Their titles—*Extinction of Useless Lights, The Mood of Now*, say—are jokes against any viewers who might try too hard to make meaning when the paintings are meaning in themselves.

When I stand in the yard while the representative from Bigfoot Pumping and Thawing drains the septic tank, I want a full report on the state of my plumbing. "Nothing serious," the guy assures me as he works his hose around. "Just a few solids." That's it, solids. I'm looking for solids. I think this matters. I'm looking for solids, lumpy shapes that will become somehow meaningful. I persist in the belief that the mind is capable of taking itself by surprise again and again, thinking new, fresh thoughts, at least new and fresh to me—and possibly to others. Who can know?

When I was an undergraduate, I spent the better part of a summer reading Beckett's great trilogy, *Molloy, Malone Dies,* and *The Unnamable,* in a Grove/Black Cat edition with eye-burningly small print. Determined to soldier through, I realized only later, rereading in bits and pieces, that in many places these books were funny—funny in a special sort of way. Molloy shifts his sucking stones from certain pockets in his greatcoat to his mouth, back to certain pockets. Not exactly a Sisyphean labor, but in the ballpark if you look at it in the right way, a kind of struggle with the question of how to be alone with yourself, with the question of how to fill your life in the face of the howling void.

One of my professors from graduate school days had a serious drinking problem. When he turned up for writers' workshops drunk, he'd wail to us: "We all die alone." One of the women in the class, whose problem was pills, would wail back, "Why, John, why?" I don't know why, either, but I do think we die as we pretty much live, alone.

When I am in a running race, a ski marathon, or on a century bike ride, despite being in the presence of others I am essentially alone. Once here in Fairbanks I found both my hamstring muscles cramping in the last ten kilometers of the Sonot Kkaazoot, a fifty-kilometer ski event. I could see my fellow SCUM Dave Bloom suffering in much the same way. But seeing his pain did nothing to alleviate mine, did nothing to make my own struggle to the finish any easier. I have never asked Dave whether my presence did anything to help him along. To do so would be out of character.

What do people think when they see a moose browsing along a road or trail on a cold day deep in winter? Do they think, say, that this animal is unhappy out there? That it is lonely? There is no getting around the fact that the moose is alone, but it's we people who too often think of being alone as a desolate state, that being alone is in itself an unhappy way to be, "so lonesome I could cry," as Hank Williams put it.

Recently, the famous sociobiologist E. O. Wilson was on the radio extolling the virtues of ants. Ants may be the most socially connected of all animal species, and, E. O. Wilson would say, one of the most successful. *Why*, he wondered, *were there not more species behaving like ants?*

I have had varieties of moose encounters on the trails. Like me, their habits are irregular; they prowl the trails by day and night. Once, on the Baseline, a narrow, rarely traveled trail, I passed a cow lounging in the snow; she hardly gave me a glance. Once I encountered one on the university's Beaver Slide Trail; she turned toward me, laid her ears back, put her hackles up, and lowered her head, making it clear I could not pass. I turned and went back the way I came. Moose don't much like my headlamp; it sometimes makes them bolt. Most of the time, though, moose go their way and I go mine, each of us alone with our thoughts.

If we are not knowable even to ourselves, my errands into the wilderness wherein I seek to know must only alienate me more from the rest of the group. *Why*, I wonder, *can't I be like an ant instead of a moose?*

In our town, there is a man who lately can be seen trudging up and down Farmers' Loop Road or University Avenue with four shopping carts. In each he has built a tall cardboard tower. Who can know what he has inside them? But one by one, or sometimes two by two, he pushes his carts along. I may see him sitting beside the four all neatly aligned; I may see him pushing one to meet the others as if he is continually making and remaking a train. Not so different from Molloy's sucking stones in his greatcoat pockets.

In much the same way, each Beckett narrator from Molloy to Malone, to the Unnamable himself in his urn set on a bar, often surrounded by others, always ignored, is not always alone but is always alone. Each man is charged with the same chore we all have been given, to make a meaningful world—out of what? The contents of our own heads?

Those are the lumps, misshapen only if we attempt to assign them recognizable shapes. Stray thoughts are shapeless. If we invent names for what they are, haven't we achieved a kind of freedom?

Some may believe in the talking cure, but I believe in the walking cure, or more specifically the skiing cure. Peace is best found through movement. Kick and glide, my pole snapping out of my hand and back again, the steady rhythm that scarcely alters at all except on the steepest hills. It is while striding that I find myself clipping off the kilometers, traveling stretches of trail with no later recollection of having passed over them at all. Surely I did; otherwise, how could I be here now?

In better times I think bigger, happier thoughts, thoughts that may carry me far away from myself and these ski trails. Some of these thoughts slip out, but they slip out the way air can be carefully released from a filled balloon. The rest evaporate, sublimate, dissolve. They are gone. Even those I've selected to save, trivial and profound, will be gone by the time I put my skis in my ski bag, climb in my truck, and go home. And the rest, those I might commit to paper or a computer disk? When I am gone, will they go with me? Be just as lost?

I do think it is possible to use exercise to wrestle the mind to exhaustion from time to time. It is possible to stay out skiing long enough, to find myself so far from the ski hut or my truck that I have to concentrate on every stride to get myself back, concentrate on the downhills especially, since nothing is worse than falling at this point. Every bit of energy I have left will simply drain into the ground. When I do fall, I lie there on the snow thinking of nothing except how to untangle my skis and poles, shift myself around and get up. In this strange way, I have achieved a kind of tranquillity, the mind finally at rest, empty.

There is some of this fear of losing everything meaningful in Beckett's narrators, maybe in Beckett himself. Words are frail, words are nothing. But if anything can, words will save us from nothingness.

Montaigne's essay "Of Idleness" ends with a little joke against his readers and, on reflection, himself: he says of his "chimeras and fantastic monsters, . . . in order to contemplate their ineptitude and strangeness at my pleasure, I have begun to put them in writing, hoping in time to make my mind ashamed of itself."

That's the trick, the joke both Beckett and Montaigne are in on. Thoughts find some sort of order once they are consigned to words on a page. No matter how baggy and rambling Montaigne's thoughts may seem to be, no matter how desolate Beckett's narrators' stories may be, they represent the mediated word. As Montaigne would have it, if not a cultivated field, at least a carefully weeded one. No matter how disparate my own words seem when committed to the page, they have more order than my rambling night-ski thoughts. We've all picked; we've all chosen. While I can't speak for Beckett or Montaigne, for me it may be a small victory, but it's all I've got.

Mont Sainte-Victoire,
Approximately

(1) Out on Schoodic Point, the plein air painters are working, canvases clamped to easels so that they might not blow into the ocean, clever devices unfolded to hold their paints, their brushes, and sometimes their rear ends. The painters position themselves close enough to feel the ocean's spray. Surrounded by nature, won't they replicate nature more fully?

Once when I went fishing with my pals O'Neill and Paulson down on the Gulkana River just north of Glennallen, Alaska, I broke my fly rod ten minutes after we got there. This was not good. We had walked about a mile and a half through bog and bugs thick enough to require that we wear headnets and long sleeves all buttoned up on a hot summer day. Still, the mosquitoes drummed against us like a soft dry rain. Down on the river the bug situation was a little better. I got my fly stuck on the bottom and while I was wrestling with the rod, whipping and yanking and cussing, it broke right at the joint between the butt and the second section.

A fishing fly is much easier to replace than a rod section, especially when you build both yourself. With my pocketknife, a stick, and duct tape, I tried to fix the rod to make it in some way fishable, but did little good. So I walked upriver to a place where I thought the water might be low enough and close enough that I could just swing a fly into the current. Somewhere on my walk I lost the tip of the rod.

A fishing rod at such a time is very like a stick. The blank it was made from was brown, a deep chocolate brown, a brown that had found a way to blend right in with all the branches that had fallen to the ground. But I'd wrapped the rod in bright orange and light blue. As I walked that bit of path, maybe a quarter-mile long, certainly less than a half, I kept thinking the orange and blue would jump out at me; I'd find the rod tip. I did not.

A fishing rod is not a stick. A fishing rod is more highly evolved, first a stick turned into a tool, a tool that resembles a stick, but one that gets further and further away from the stick it came from. My stick was graphite, a hollow graphite tube covered on the outside by brown heat-shrunk cellophane. The wraps and guides—put on last and what most made it a tool for fishing—were secured with a couple of coats of epoxy. My stick was a product of our technological age gone missing in the natural world.

◆ ◆ ◆

Years ago, when I was driving to Alaska for the first time, I stopped to camp in Banff, Alberta. In the morning, out for a jog, I passed under the great rocky faces of the mountains above me. It was a view that might set a person thinking of Paul Cézanne and of the many paintings he did of the same scene, Mont Sainte-Victoire. What was he trying to get at there? Certainly, the view of the mountain changed every day as Cézanne repositioned himself; it changed with the seasons, changed with the quality of light, changed subtly geologically, and changed most importantly with the frame of mind of the painter. What I see when I look at these paintings are the hard planes that slam together to make a mountain, that give it body and mass as it pushes up out of the plain. What I see is what I saw in Banff, that a mountain is made of rock, and rock insists on possessing its place. It is stronger than we are and older and will surely outlast us.

What, I think, was his point? The piece of fishing rod still lost in the woods down by the Gulkana River and Cézanne's many paintings of Mont Sainte-Victoire, of still lifes of bowls of apples and pears are stuck in that awkward in-between place where we live out our lives, the natural world and the human-made world we have tried to build on top of it.

In the funny papers these days, Zippy the Pinhead concurs. Early in the summer the strip announces, "Proof the World Is Triangular." At the beach, Zippy lounges under a grass shack with a pyramidal roof. "It's just *me*, th' gentle, lapping waves & th' *eternal now* . . ."

Cézanne got into a similar place himself. The cylinder, the sphere, the cone. These were not the shapes the world was made of; these were the shapes a painter might apply to the world to bring it to terms on his canvas. When I consider this idea, I think of the Saturday morning TV show from my boyhood, *Learn to Draw* with Jon Gnagy, a real artist with a goatee and everything. As a sprightly waltz played in the background, the voice-over announced that if we could draw a triangle, a circle, and a square, we could learn to draw. Sometimes my brother and I would race for pieces of paper and pencils. We didn't intend to prove Jon Gnagy wrong, but it always came out that way.

What art critic Clement Greenberg would like to say is that what happened in the transformation of Mont Sainte-Victoire into Cézanne's favorite shapes was mostly in the mind of the painter, that what happened when Cézanne tried to catch the mountain on canvas was a demonstration of an obvious truth: you can't cram three dimensions into two. People always knew that, really, in the way that dogs and cats know that pictures of dogs, cats, and food are not the real deal. Some great leap of faith happened in our childhood brains when we looked in the mirror and at pictures of ourselves and decided to agree that they were us.

Now digital cameras have been developed that will break an image into more than ten thousand dots per square inch. By breaking the world into ever smaller bits, perhaps we hope to possess its beauty. The eye cannot detect this artifice. My ear cannot detect the artifice of digitalized music, of breaking sustained tones into bits. I am not sure anybody's can, but I know musicians who find digitalization a troublesome problem.

In this way, the story of Achilles and the tortoise can be seen as a fable of imitation. People may aspire to imitate the natural world; we may get closer and closer but we never seem to get there. In the last panel of his triangular adventure, Zippy hollers, "Hey! Would somebody please adjust the horizon line?!" There's the truth; the earth just curves right out from under us. The world won't sit still for our wishes very long. We may understand this idea best through mathematics.

(2) Some mornings I wake up frightened and angry. I am afraid I am going to die, not right away, but soon enough, too soon, and I am angry that I'm not doing anything about it. I want to punch something or somebody. I mean to say, I am wasting my life.

O'Neill, Paulson, and I had come to the lower Gulkana to catch salmon, chinook salmon or at least a few sockeye. These salmon had found their way back to this river from the great ocean, up through Prince William Sound and the Copper River. Some say they smell their way home, but people don't really know for sure how fish know what they know. And I wonder often if such fish ever fail to run up the right river and just make do with the river they have wandered into. To make more salmon and die is what they've come for. Up on the bank, we like to think we understand their imperatives more clearly than they do.

We do insofar as we have made up names for some of them. "Beasts abstract not." I went around for years thinking Ovid said that, maybe in *The Metamorphoses*, but it was John Locke instead. Too bad, because it's in *The Metamorphoses* that all sorts of unfortunate people and even some minor gods and demigods get turned into plants, animals, and heavenly bodies. I guess when it happens, when a person turns into a tree as Daphne does or a spider as Arachne does, she lets go of abstract thought then and there.

I am inclined to believe the natural world means nothing, literally nothing, unless people are around to give it a name, to give it meaning. Come with me again to walk through the woods looking for my lost rod tip. We are well away from the highway; we are in Alaska, a state where moose still outnumber human beings. We are in a fishing spot Paulson has made us swear never to reveal to others. Yet plenty of others have been here. The little trail I follow on the bluff above the river has not been made by meandering animals but by purposeful humans going upriver to the next good fishing spot. And as I look for the orange and blue bands of the rod tip, other bits of color imported into the natural world jump out at me: soda cans, bubble packaging for fishing lures, bits of surveyor's tape, wads of monofilament fishing line, a bright yellow piece of broken shoelace.

This litter serves as a system of markers as I try to organize my search for the rod tip. Scattered among the many constellations of cottonwood and birch trees with different configurations of branches, but trees still more alike than not, this human trash becomes my template, my order I overlay on the natural world. Often I find on the rivers I fish arrangements of sticks, stacks of rocks, cuts in tree bark—other humans' codes laid over a nature with secret codes of its own. I have some surveyor's tape in one of my fishing vest pockets for this very purpose of making nature more orderly on my terms. I cannot help but do this.

When I hold a thrashing salmon in my net and raise my club to end its life, there I see, as its flat eye twitches around for something to grab on to, an awareness. Something, again, it cannot name but knows. I think about this awareness when I see a road kill, a possum, a raccoon, a squirrel. I think about it even more if the dead animal is a dog or cat, since I sentimentally persist in believing I know their thoughts better. What I do know is that such animals were sentient; they could and did solve rudimentary problems.

In some important ways, their senses had been more alive to the world than ours can ever be. Beginning with the salmon, they all could smell their way home. And in an instant, they are no more. They are returned to matter.

Clement Greenberg saw in Cézanne the birth of modernism. Beginning with that first step, the imposition of form on the natural world, you could make Greenberg's argument work. And would it lead you out at modernism's logical end? That end might be the primacy of art over the objects of the world. Art: the imposition of our human sense of beauty and order on what's already out there? Art: the recognition of the distance that always stands between us and the natural world?

Once, back in Virginia, my boyhood neighbor Mr. Mullin gave me a fishing fly when he came back from Dismal Creek. The Bearman Fly he called it; the Bearman himself had given it to him. I pictured this Bearman as a cross between an old-time mountaineer and a spirit, somebody who knew the woods because he had seemingly lived in them forever. The Bearman Fly was a little bit of nothing: some fine yellow chenille wound on a hook with a brown hackle palmered through the top third. That's all. Years later, I appreciated it more. The Bearman Fly looks almost like a lot of bugs in a river that a trout might eat.

Whatever a brushstroke is, this is what it is not: a rock, an ocean wave, the skin of a pear. Every map we make, every picture we attempt from the natural world is an overlay, a human ordering of a world that would be doing just fine without us. Maybe this is why the fishing flies I like the best are those that don't look like any bug or fish in particular. In these flies there is a recognition that although we belong to nature, we have our little moments when we slide up and away from it.

Math might be a language that existed before people knew it, before we discovered our need for it. Pi seems to work this way. There was a pi before people found it hidden in an equation, always there, knowable, usable, but impossible to know absolutely. Two kooky Russian brothers have hooked a whole roomful of personal computers together and attempted to solve for pi. After millions of digits, they have come to no neat end, not even to a repeated pattern. Maybe, they think, in some mathematical-mystical way this proves the existence of God. I wonder if the opposite might be the case. Math may be a part of the natural world, or it may belong to us.

◆ ◆ ◆

Outside, the wind is whipping and driving rain against the windows. I am thinking of a picture in a book of a man in a sea kayak running up and over a wave, his paddle pointed ahead of him like a lance. After being cooped up by the rain all day, I feel I would like to be that man; I would like to take out the kayak stored in the basement and run through the waves, to risk flipping over in the cold ocean.

Eventually, Clement Greenberg says, painters would cut themselves loose from the need to abstract art from the world. Cézanne had painted the same mountain over and over again to mine a harder meaning out of it, to carry it away from nature. He did the same with pieces of fruit. I would like to think he was trying to bring out beauty, to give it a name, name it through paint. And in his naming it, would we all come to own it?

Note from a day of fishing: twice I have slipped, once sliding off a rock in midstream and catching myself with both hands, wetting my sleeves to the elbows. My rod has clattered into the water, but it is shallow in this spot and I retrieve it easily. The second time, I've skidded down a gravelly bank and landed on my rump. A few days later, riding in the car, I will notice a deep bruise in my hip joint from this fall, but I have fished on. And to show for my day on two different creeks, one small seven- or eight-inch fish, a fish foolish enough to rise to a newfangled fly its creator calls a Purple Haze. We push on nature and nature pushes back.

On this rainy day, I reconsider, ask myself if it isn't better to settle for being cooped up in the house. The ocean heaves against the rocks outside the window, carrying them off bit by bit. Inside, we have the illusion of life steady and safe. As I write, I can smell the cheesy smell of my bare feet under the desk. That smell comes from the dead flesh on my heels and big toes. No, it's not, it's the smell of the bacteria eating away at the dead flesh on my feet, it's the smell of their by-product: the ordinary smell of death.

People who don't like abstract art sometimes think of it as a cosmic giving up, but we might better think of it as a more aggressive assault by people on what's really there. Before people figured out how to draw perspective to imply distance, Egyptians did it by just drawing any number of horizon lines one above the other. The higher the line, the farther away the people and objects on that line were understood to be. Not a very precise way of getting at depth perception, but the people looking at the drawings understood it. They understood it as symbol, a symbol that fits awkwardly over the world.

Here is what I know about myself. I cannot fully live unless I get the kayak out and paddle out into the ocean. Some days I crave the ocean most when the weather is stinky, the bay choppy, the breeze stiff, the sun hidden by heavy banks of clouds.

In Hans Namuth's short film of Jackson Pollock at work, the artist moves like a big caged cat above a pane of glass standing in place of a canvas. In his Red Wing work boots, he strides around the edges of his work, paint can in one hand and brush in the other, and I feel he would slink off into the woods and never come back if it weren't for whatever there is in the act of painting that pulls him back. Somebody resistant to Pollock's wiles might say nothing pulls him back. Nothing pulls him but color and shape, color and shape experienced so viscerally that I want to think that the way a person might understand these paintings is carried by us all down deep in our DNA.

In a beginner's book for fly tiers, I read, "The tail should be equal to the distance from the back of the eye to the start of the bend on wets and nymphs, and equal to the distance from the front of the eye to the start of the bend on dries. The body should begin at a point directly opposite the point of the barb and end halfway between the point of the hook and the back of the eye. The hackle should be 1 ½ times the gap of the hook, and the wings should be twice the gap. The head should be equal to the size of the eye."

Nature, we suppose, is attuned to proportionality. This is the idea of the elegant equation: its truth is made all the more compelling through its grace and style. When Pythagoras came up with his theorem, it had just such elegance. Wasn't it safe to assume the whole universe would be an elegant place if we could only figure out the equations? People cling to the idea of elegance to this day.

◆ ◆ ◆

I wonder how many people, when thinking about Cézanne's great paintings, think of the man himself, lonely, isolated from other artists off in Paris, and human. Here he is working in plein air, in the natural world, when he could have done otherwise. Here he is in coat and tie. His ideas seem to lead his painting; he could easily have jumped away from recognizable subjects from where he stood. It would have been a short jump.

Some days I resign myself to going down into the basement and riding a stationary bicycle. Forty-five minutes is about all I can manage at stiff resistance. To pass the time, I break forty-five into fifteenths, fifths, thirds, quarters, and ninths. Here is the funny thing about ninths: each one from one to eight is a repeating decimal, an infinitely repeating decimal. Each is a little like pi, only neater. Each will go on forever in its own direction, a branch off the infinite progression of whole numbers, what we call natural numbers.

Cézanne did not jump. Maybe he couldn't. Despite his ideas about cylinders, spheres, and cones, ideas designed to release him into pure form, he remained tethered to the earth. How far can the world be stretched toward our sense of beauty and still be what it seems? How far can we lean away from that world and still know who we are? Cézanne's refusal seems as much a source of emotional power in his work as does his struggle with color and shape.

Across the road from the driveway lies a dead animal. Is it a rat or a squirrel? I go over to inspect. Its body is shabby and black, its mouth cocked open baring its small worn teeth. *It's a squirrel,* I think, and think again, *What difference does it make now?* We can imagine a perfect circle, but we cannot draw one. So when we die, what becomes of pi? Here is an idea in the world, an idea that will outlive us, that makes the world make sense, yet it seems to live only in our human heads. The dead squirrel in the gutter knew nothing of it.

Painting and writing—thinking, too—are ways of knowing who we are. But they don't stop the inevitable from happening. If we are not the critter stepping out from among the corn rows into the path of the tractor-trailer, we are the one who stands up in the boat to pee and pitches over the side, the one who bicycles on the too-narrow road, the one who drinks too much or eats himself into obesity, the one who has the bad genetic luck to have a malformed heart, the one whose cells finally just grow weary of replication.

The other day out shopping, I looked up from a rack of tie-dyed T-shirts and saw a kid standing by the cash register chatting up the help. He cheerfully wore a spiked and peroxided Mohawk twenty years past its headbanging moment. On the green baseball-sleeve shirt he wore, he'd scrawled in Magic Marker, "I'm an animal." *A tame, well-fed animal,* I thought, and as he walked away, I saw the slogan on his back, "And so are you." The kid and I: we are both animals, and we will die as surely as the squirrel did.

When Jackson Pollock jumped, jumped all the way into the purest kind of art, where was there for him to land safely? I don't think he ever found his landing place. Not even in his crash-destroyed car.

I still have my Bearman Fly after almost forty years. I admire it, and I believe in what it stands for. I like the Adams, the Woolly Bugger, the Hare's Ear as well. I like them because, like the Bearman Fly, they say to nature, We know your game. We see your game and we know a little bit of how it works. And these flies say, We people have a little game of our own going, too.

There is a way that art, my art anyway, even the small offhand art of tying a fly, wants to bounce back and forth between what is living and what is not. The old-time fishing flies were mostly made of formerly living things—bits of feather and fur, a little thread and sometimes a bit of tinsel. The body of the Hare's Ear nymph, with its fur spun onto thread and wrapped around a fishhook, the tinsel wound over barber-pole style, would suggest the segmented body of an aquatic insect. A folded-over piece of feather would suggest the insect's own wing case, and the wound hackle at the front of the fly, the swimming legs pawing their way to the surface as a fisher tugged the line. A crude representation at best, a compressed, generalized take on any number of bugs. A fly whose proportions are designed to please the human eye as much as the eye of a fish. Its success can be measured only by how well it actually might please the fish. And often enough it does until the fish tastes the iron of the hook.

Why make such a thing that takes its place between the real and the abstract? Maybe to achieve a state of being that isn't available to me at all. All art must wish to get up above our current selves and outlast us. To make a mark on the hardest rock, I say, to outlast pi if such a thing could be possible. I think about a smear of paint across a canvas, a series of smears, a series of drips and dribbles, and I think about how they do not come up to a representation of Mont Sainte-Victoire. I am not sure they ever can or ever need to. What I am sure of is that the kind of tension between what is and what we can understand is a running quarrel between Great Nature and me.

During the few months it has taken me to arrange these thoughts, my sometime fishing buddy Jon Paulson has been diagnosed and has died from complications of brain cancer. As the disease progressed, he forgot how to button his shirt and how to tie his shoes, but he never lost track of who he was. O'Neill and a couple of others took Paulson's ashes down to his secret spot on the Gulkana and scattered them, scattered them down where my rod tip of graphite, epoxy, and steel remains hidden in the woods.

To be in the kayak riding in the storm and comfortably in the house at the same time, to be outside time and all it stands for and yet be living here and now. That's what I'd like, that one thing. That it can't happen is maybe the cruelest trick nature must play on us. To know the infinite but not experience it, well, I have to resent that, to fight against such a circumstance however I can. My art, then, must be my resistance.

I Held Their Coats

A Study of Two Jokes

Reader, I, too, wonder about what follows. I wonder what calls a person to think something is or is not funny. What causes us to remember some jokes and to forget others. What the simple act of remembering might mean, what it might say about who we are and what we value. So I guess I must ask your indulgence for some ugliness that follows, that you put aside your misgivings, consider it all with me and see what you think, too.

My brother and I used to sit by the living room window waiting for our uncles to come driving up the hill to our house. Often it was Thanksgiving Eve and late at night when they arrived. Living on a dead end as we did, we had no tricks to make the time go faster, no counting of makes and models of passing cars. The clock with no second hand barely crept along. Our uncles brought our cousins who, even the ones who were younger than we were, knew better, knew more. Our uncles had gone off to the bigger world, bigger towns. Our folks stayed back in the hills, up in the hollow.

Whenever these uncles came to see us, they came with a bunch of stored-up jokes to tell. They told these jokes to my parents. I don't think they were very good joke tellers; you wouldn't want to call them storytellers. My uncle Bill would just rattle them off in quick sequence: "What do you call a Chinese virgin?" Then before anybody could think: "No Yen To." "A Chinese person in Las Vegas?" . . . "Dough Gone Now." My uncles Jim and Jack tried to make a little more of a narrative of their jokes, but for all my uncles, the whole point of a joke was the punch line; the trick was to get there as quickly as you could. Their jokes might be political, topical, faddish. Sometimes they were about touchy subjects—race, say; but rarely, and then only mildly, about sex. If they offended my mother in the telling, my uncles never meant to.

Uncle Jack would plop into the red reclining chair—our dad's chair—with a certain droit de seigneur, read my dad's newspaper. Holler to my mom, "Hey, Sis, are any of my khakis still around here?"—a different kind of joke, a joke between my mom and dad. Fifteen years after the war, Uncle Jack still imagined a footlocker around the house somewhere containing a limitless supply of his soldier's khaki pants.

Here is a joke he told us:

This black guy wanted to go out for a college football team. (But Uncle Jack would have said a colored boy, and we all would have understood that the college my uncle meant was a white college, an all-white college in the South, the only kind of college any of us would have thought of. It was that time in our country's history.) Anyhow, this colored boy went up to the coach and said he wanted to play some football for him.

And the coach . . . I always pictured him as a thick-chested short man, a man in a gray sweatshirt and ball cap with a whistle on a lanyard, and probably wearing khaki pants . . . and the coach said reluctantly, grudgingly, probably embarrassed and resentful all at once, "Okay, I'll give you a try." He let the colored boy line up in the backfield with the second team and told the quarterback to give him the ball.

Sometimes I pictured the joke taking place on the lumpy football field behind our high school—the very field I practiced on all fall with my Midget football team, a field full of standing water and breeding mosquitoes on into October. Other times I pictured it happening on the lush green practice fields behind E. C. Glass High in Lynchburg, Virginia—a place where field gave onto field and where sprinklers shot rainbows of mist onto the grass every morning and evening. Uncle Jack and Aunt Mildred lived in Lynchburg, and he taught and coached at E. C. Glass.

The colored boy broke through the line and dodged his way through the secondary until he was standing all by himself in the end zone. And I saw that in my head clearly, too, the beauty of broken field running, the kind of play my dad would have called us from our attic room to look at on the TV in those days before instant replay, when we had to hurry from our homework or we'd miss it.

In those days, E. C. Glass was the biggest high school in Virginia and a major football power, always in the hunt for the Class AAA championship. They ran the antique single-wing attack, but their boys were so many, so big, it didn't much matter. When they came to Bluefield to play once, my dad and my brother and I went to see them in their royal-blue jerseys, helmets, and pants (blue pants even!), like a small army when they ran from the visitors' locker room. They had oxygen on the sidelines for their players when they came off the field. We thought it was to compensate for the higher elevation. Only later did I learn that major college teams, professional teams kept oxygen on the sidelines for every game just to give the players a lift.

Well, now. The coach told the colored boy to try it again, only this time the coach snuck over and told the first team the play. The same thing happened. The boy just ran right through the line, knocking aside the offensive and defensive players, and wound up in the end zone again. So while the boy was trotting back up the field, the coach told the second team not to block for him on the next try. It didn't matter, that boy ran right through them all again.

Race jokes were not told in our house. Once a kid friend of mine enticed me to holler up to a bunch of black kids our age walking along the back road that ran around the lip of the hollow we lived in. We stood out front of my house up under the shadows of the big maple tree and yelled, "Hey, chocolate drops, hey, little jungle bunnies," though we were all about the same first-grade size. I heard the storm door rattle open on the front porch behind me. "Bud, get in here right now," my mother told me. And when I went in, I automatically sat in one of the stuffed living room chairs to hear my scolding. The very rattle of the door had warned me.

"We don't," my mother said, "call people names because of what color their skin is. People can't help that."

My parents ran a little grocery store. Those kids' folks were our customers. The kids themselves were our customers, standing by the big windows at the front of the store waiting for the bus that would take them to the one consolidated school for all the black kids in the county. They bought blow gum and licorice whips and gingersnaps just like the white kids who came through the store later. When I got big enough to carry a box of groceries, I would help deliver orders to their houses. And later, when integration finally came, they would be my classmates, my bandmates, my teammates.

Lynchburg had a high school for black kids too: Dunbar. "The Poets," my aunt hooted. "They call themselves the Poets." I pictured a black kid in his varsity jacket. There would have to be a quill pen on it somewhere, a pen sticking out of an inkwell. I pictured a kind of style that went with being a poet, berets and sunglasses, a looseness in the walk. It wasn't such a terrible thing to be. Later, my mother said there was a colored man poet, that's who that school was named for, she bet. I can't guess how my mom ran across Paul Laurence Dunbar—possibly in the inspirational literature for her Sunday school class—but it was just like her to take this kind of corrective action, to worry out an explanation, get to the truth of the matter regardless of how long it took. And I could tell by the way she let us in on this information that she expected us to put it together and see the various ways my aunt had got it wrong. A poet was a perfectly good mascot.

Finally it came down to the colored boy on one side of the ball all by himself and the first-team defense arrayed against him. And there he went running through the line and into the secondary, running and stiff-arming and dodging his way to another touchdown.

The coach threw down his hat and hollered, "Hoo whee, look at that Polynesian boy run."

My parents laughed at my uncle's joke. It was a funny joke. I still think it's a funny joke. When I was a boy I told it over and over to myself, refining my uncle's details, making it richer, making the number of steps the boy had to go through longer and more complicated.

Coaches rarely appreciate an ironic sensibility. The ironist is never exactly where you think he is. His body is right there in front of you, but his thoughts have wandered off to fix you from some altogether different angle. Not a very useful trait for any kind of ballplayer. So it was that as I grew, an absent-minded ballplayer, an ironist in training, I wondered how my uncle could tell his race joke and never see how it came back around on him: the only part for him to play, an assistant football coach at an all-white school.

My mother would say of just about anybody who didn't get a joke, "He's just like an Englishman." I don't know how she could have run across any such humorless Englishman in our hometown to test this theory out, but the upshot of it was that you had to explain a joke to such a person, and nothing ruined a joke worse than having to explain it. I guess I've come to the explaining part of this joke. I've come to try to explain it because I wonder why of the many jokes I've heard and forgotten, I've kept this one in my head so long.

Here is how the Commonwealth of Virginia finally came to accommodate racial integration: gently, apologetically, and with the greatest possible resistance. While down in Alabama, Bull Connor turned loose the police dogs and the fire hoses, the good people of Virginia just said, "No, thank you." That was how you turned away an encyclopedia salesman, a Jehovah's Witness who came to your door. There was no need to be rude. People with good manners always knew when they weren't wanted.

Robert E. Lee, for instance, was always a gentleman. He loved his men and he loved his horse Traveler. He shook hands in defeat. Most likely, our grade-school teachers assured us, he would have freed his slaves anyway.

And when Virginia's time came, why, like a rich old lady who gets things a little bit mixed up from time to time, but who has the right granted her age and her standing to always have it her way, things would just be different from here on out without ever having to admit the way they had been was wrong. All the little Polynesian boys and girls would take their places in the clarinet section of the band, in English class and math and chemistry, and on the football team. Sometimes in the backfield.

A friend of mine told me a story of winning a long-distance footrace at a Boy Scouts jamboree. The racecourse took him past the camps of the black Scout troops. When he finished the race, he wondered out loud why the black Scouts had not been allowed into the competitions. "Son," a Scout leader told him, "if those boys were in this race, you wouldn't have won it." That's the other part of the joke.

Maybe that's the ugliest part, the part about being afraid of what integration would bring. The black players would run through the white players even when the white players knew the play. Black people would overpower white people. Animal strength would win out over mere entitlement every time. That was another category of race joke, the kind you'd not hear my uncle tell in my parents' house because he'd know better, a race joke about the sexual prowess of black men or black women or both. Those jokes were supposed to scare you. Maybe my uncle's football joke was, too, but only in a glancing way. The black player had both skills and courage. I admired him; he was the football player I wanted to be but couldn't.

I knew white players who had skill and courage. A fullback named Gerald Perez who would catch a kickoff and stand for a moment with the ball resting on his hip, looking over the onrushing opponents, looking for the best way to run through them.

Others, too, skinny quarterbacks and tailbacks who threw their whole bodies flying into blocks. Guards and tackles too frail for their positions, but fierce. Those who would get into fistfights only to ease the pain of losing.

The black and white boys I played with had some fistfights too. Robert Howell and William Johnson, one white forward, one black, had a fight at basketball practice just about once a week. Race had something to do with these fights, but not nearly everything. Race was the easiest thing to call it, and sometimes still is.

And that might be the saddest part of the joke. How we never really accommodated race, how we used words to hide from the problem. How the black player got on the team, but without the team ever accepting who he really was.

I am getting closer to understanding why I like this joke. Because it is funny, because it is ugly, because it is sad. Because racism in America and in the South in particular is such a long and complicated story, and this joke balls so much of it all up in a tight little package I can carry around and remember. I can pull it out and tell it to myself from time to time, tell it to my friends. Because we will be driving along in the car and something will come on the radio, some part of the O. J. Simpson mess, say, and I will tell this joke as a way of getting at what it is I think.

Except all that leaves a lot unexplained. For example, what responsibility, culpability even, could I have for carrying this joke around all these years? What made me remember it, and what does that say about me? Would I be ashamed if, under anesthetic, I suddenly came out with this joke in a hospital operating room? Hospitals may be the most integrated workplaces in this country. That is where I was, on my way to visit my dad in the ICU, when the O. J. verdict was announced. Everybody froze. I froze, even though it took some bit of time out of my ten minutes allotted to visit with Dad. And at that moment, the racial divisiveness of our culture was never more apparent. The black people sighed and let themselves smile small smiles. No high fives, no laughter, this was relief, this was getting out from under some implicit collective guilt. And the white people tried not to look disgusted at what they saw as the injustice of it all. Where was that Polynesian boy then?

Or years from now as a dotty old man will I sit in the sun at the old folks' home and pop out with this joke, pop out with it to one of the black minimum-wage employees who seem to be the heart and soul of every old folks' home I've set foot in? What has made me carry this joke around, allowed me to roll it around in my head the way I roll around a Life Saver in my mouth, savoring it, playing with it? Mostly I have allowed myself to stand aside, to mock old Virginia, to place blame as if I had never been an enfranchised citizen of that green commonwealth. At the most, I have let the joke be about us, and who am I but the smallest droplet in an ocean of us? What does this joke say about me?

Because here is an uglier joke, a joke about sex, not race. This is a joke that I am not sure is funny at all. This is a joke that I would be happy to have out of my head if it would just go, but like an annoying jingle, there it is, popping into my thoughts. Unbidden, it comes to me; there is never a right time for it. It is more like a sore in my mouth that my tongue can't stay away from. A joke my uncles would never tell and that would cause my mother to cover her ears in shame.

A man goes to a whorehouse. He asks for the ugliest, skinniest whore in the house, and he is led to a dark basement room where a lonely, pimply whore is shivering naked under a moth-eaten army blanket. He pays his money and tells the whore to take off the blanket and lie there. Then he straddles her and shits on her. "Now, don't move," he tells her and leaves.

I am not exactly sure where I first heard this joke. At band camp, I think. I started going to band camp before I was even old enough to be in band. My dad took a whole truckload of groceries over to this camp, rented from the Boy Scouts, and when I saw the cabins and the creek, I wanted to stay. And he let me, my folks bringing back a suitcase of clothes for me later that night. Actually, it was no fun at all. I didn't know any of these older kids, and I was lonely as hell.

Odd things went on at band camp. At night, the chaperones and the band director retreated to the staff cabin and drank, I suppose. And we had the run of the place. Here's a representative moment. A boy called Larry, maybe four or five years older than I, is up on a top bunk in one of the boys' cabins where he's fashioned a kind of stage with a curtain made from several of our blankets thrown over the rafters. He parts the curtain, steps through, and begins to do a striptease, peeling off his T-shirt and briefs. Somehow he has managed to tuck his penis between his legs and keep it there as he does his bump and grind. I have never seen a woman naked below the waist; I don't know what I am supposed to be looking at. But along with the other boys, I sit on the lower bunks and hoot and whistle just like I'd be expected to do in a real strip club, a place I am certain none of us had ever been.

Here is something I do know, even at this age. The bizarre goings-on at band camp are to go in a separate drawer in my memory. They are not to be shared with the other kids who didn't go. They are not to be recounted, reconsidered—even among the kids who were there. Certainly, they aren't for Mom.

Either at band camps or at real Scout camps in the same location, I would fill plastic bags with piss and throw them at other campers. Examine my first condom, unrolling it, inspecting it, rolling it back up, but not trying it on. Participate reluctantly in a circle jerk. Look at dirty magazines and hear stories read from them with frighteningly unlikely anatomical details—a woman, driven by guilt after a moment of lesbian sex, throws herself from a high window; when she hits the sidewalk below, her breasts burst like cartons of milk.

There is an initiation into the world of men. Here is how you pass the test: (1) don't blab, (2) don't ask questions, (3) pass it on.

Who was I when I was this boy who sat around a campfire as it burned down to its embers listening (avidly listening) to such stories and jokes? I am thinking now of the stoning of Stephen, how it all came about from his telling a group of men something they didn't want to hear, that Jesus was the son of God. Enough was enough; they started throwing rocks. Off to the side is the figure who interests me most: Paul, still going by Saul, holds the men's coats for them while the deed is done. What does feeling ashamed of what we see before us have to do with our complicity?

The whore, the whore in the joke, is still lying on her poor cot when the man comes back the next day, climbs up over her and again shits, tells her not to move, and leaves.

I would like to believe I have a pretty normal life after being exposed to a boyhood full of polymorphously perverse behavior. Despite all the jokes about impossibly long dicks going into and out of women in wildly improbable places, about exploding jockstraps, about rape and mayhem practiced against women who never seemed to mind it so very much, I want to hope I have managed not to grow into a hateful, predaceous man. If it is so, it may be because I failed to learn the lessons of my initiation.

I was innocent then, not just of sex, but of the kind of responsibility I wonder if you don't take just by standing around the way men do when they tell dirty jokes, heads bent toward the ground, ears cocked toward the teller, knowing grins of anticipation on their faces. There is a kind of naughty playfulness in sex that is a fine and wonderful thing. Listening to a nicer kind of dirty joke might sometimes be akin to that, something edgy, sexy, and yet seeking to do no harm. I know a joke about a monkey, an elephant, and a Corvette that works that way. But a mean joke like this one requires of us a kind of bonding up, a way of listening without looking one another in the eye. The world is full of bad behavior, and a joke is one way we come to know about it.

From the moment I came back from that first band camp, a kind of separation between my parents and me began that could only deepen. As it must. At some level, it is a not-so-bad thing. It is part of a scheme of things that would take me down a road so far that eventually I would somehow be able to come back to my mom later, as an adult, a different person than she; and part of that difference would be in the things we would know.

And would part of it be the things we must hide from each other? Only once in my life have I had sex with a woman who was merely an acquaintance. I have loved the women I slept with, and I think I've tried for the kind of intimacy that female friends assure me is a necessary prelude to sex for them. I would like to say me, too. I love women; I love to look at them in all shapes and sizes. I enjoy them much more than men in conversation and would like to think my sexual relationships with them are a part of a much more complicated and rich interaction. I don't look at girlie magazines and I don't traffic much in dirty jokes in my adult life.

Here I am blabbing.

When I was an eighth grader, a ceremony of initiation went on in the band room. It was fifth period, when those of us in band were yanked out of study hall to try to practice as a small cobbled-together group. Sometimes, far too often it seemed to me, the band director went into the teachers' lounge and smoked or stayed in the cafeteria and talked to the guidance counselor. Then the upperclassmen took me and another eighth grader and pushed us into the instrument room, came in behind us, and turned out the light. Our job was to get out of the room any way we could, theirs was to whale on us with drumsticks.

It didn't matter whether you were the one trying to get out of the room or the one holding the drumstick. What mattered was that we were all in on it. I learned some things in the instrument room. I learned I could take a blow without crying out. And in that first year of high school I learned I could take any number of blows and jokes and teasing at my expense. I think that's what I was supposed to learn.

When the time came I was to pass on the lesson. But I didn't; I didn't and I couldn't. I wasn't sure what I should do, and I still am not.

What I do is wonder. I wonder about this dirty joke and what it says about men and women, what it was supposed to teach the boy who heard it when he had only the vaguest notion of the biomechanics of any sexual act, when he could not explain what it was a whore did exactly. When he understood only one part of the joke clearly: shit.

Camps had outhouses and only outhouses then. And the campers, as part of their camper chores, dumped cans of lime down them every day, swept them assiduously. The outhouses made you think about excretion more, even more than boys normally think about such bodily functions. You smelled your shit, you heard the gentle thud it made at the bottom of the dark earthen shaft. You tried experiments passed along by camp folklorists—a firecracker down the hole in the seat just to see if it really would blow up the shack.

So I thought of the whore lying in her bed as the man in the joke came back day after day and shat on her. A huge mound of shit was building on her just as it built up in the outhouse, and I saw it in mixed colors—deep brown, green, maroon, ocher, burnt umber, burnt and raw sienna. All mixed together and finally blending together as it rotted. And the stink? Beyond my imagining. I thought of stinky things I knew—rotten potatoes, dead possums on the roadside—it would be worse than any of that.

We are coming toward the punch line. When the punch line comes, men break apart like a rack of pool balls, laughing. Apart, distancing themselves from the teller. It's behavior that's as old as Adam.

So one day the guy comes back, and he climbs up on his huge pile of shit and he strains and strains, and nothing happens. And he goes away.

The woman waits. She is at the man's disposal. Like a figure in an existential novel, she is trapped in her waiting; there seems to be no way for her to eat or drink or to take a shit herself if she needs to. She waits. There is something in the sheer force of the simplest narrative that makes us wait, too, wait without giving much thought to whatever improbabilities are bound up in the situation. Once, at a younger stage in my writing, I thought a story should work like a freight train, like the freight trains that ran through my college town in the middle of the night. Guys I knew would get high and go down to the railroad tracks and try to stand inches away as the train rushed past. A story could work like that, I thought. And if you let it, it will. It will just blow on by and leave without ever offering an explanation.

This is not the kind of fun, naughty joke like the one about the monkey, the elephant, and the Corvette, which I am not going to tell you. This is a hurtful joke, isn't it? This is a simple joke that says women are shit, should be treated like shit, and they really even like to be treated like shit. There is no chance for the woman to be resourceful or brave like the colored boy. There is only the end, when the guy comes back again for several days running, constipated, unable to add to his pile. Discouraged, he climbs off and starts out of the room.

There is a movement under the pile. As a kid, I pictured this, pictured what has been a gloppy mass of shit suddenly transformed into something like Lincoln Logs, discrete woodlike turds that begin a rumbling little landslide as the whore begins to raise herself up out of the pile.

"What's the matter," she asks, "don't you love me anymore?"

I have been able to tell this joke aloud only a time or two in my life, such is my terror of it. Yet the last time I did, to a woman I love dearly, I burst into laughter at the punch line. What kind of laughter was that? I am still not sure I know. Was it an outrush of embarrassment? Was it a kind of recognition of the self that has carried this ugly thing around so long inside me? Was it an apology, a way of saying, "Listen, it's not as bad as you think"?

Recently, in a big town near where I live, a little girl was walking home from school when a man in a blue pickup truck pulled alongside her and offered her a ride. She told him "No, thank you," and he drove on. But he came back, and he forced the little girl into his truck, took her to a woody spot, and raped her. Then she somehow managed to get away.

I think about this moment because I know why she turned down the ride. Her mother told her what all our mothers told us, never to accept rides with strangers. I have a good friend who as a little girl accepted such a ride just to find out why. Nothing happened except she got spanked by her mom and by her dad, too, when he got home. I think about what her parents knew, what all our moms knew, all our moms who told us never to accept rides with strangers. What they knew was all about the ugly filth down inside the sewer pipes running below the sunny world we walk on and what might spew out if we chanced to pry the lids off. In other words, there is nothing in any dirty joke that in some vague form or another a mom has not forced herself to imagine.

What every joke needs is somebody to tell it and somebody to listen, somebody to listen and pass it on. But what, exactly, do jokes such as these bring us to? Shame and grief? Despair? Confusion about what one ought to do in this life, in this world? A comeuppance served with a dash of surprise? An acknowledgment of unjust things? A way not to get so angry? A good kick in the ass? A way to give or take away some hurt? A way of ganging up against somebody? A way to know ourselves and the world we live in more truly? A safe way to say things?

What was my female friend to think? And what do you think, reader? Maybe jokes are little explosions like the kind we boys expected when we threw the firecracker down the outhouse hole. I think sometimes the jokes we keep, what somebody might want to call the best jokes and somebody else might call the worst, are full of truths so ugly we'd better laugh. Otherwise, what would we do?

A Little Iliad

When I was a boy, I wasn't very brave. In my head, I saw myself as a quick halfback, what my dad called a "scat back," racing around the end, straight-arming some onrushing tacklers as I turned upfield toward the goal line, and just outrunning the rest of the defense. I had a compressed, sturdy, muscular body. I was fierce. The problem was, I had constructed a cartoon version of my long, bony self that was not really me at all. In my daydreams, the jarring contact that marks the end of nearly every run a halfback makes was fleeting and incidental. Possessed of speed and grace, I had no need to crash into anybody.

Boyhood as practiced in Pocahontas, Virginia, was all about bravery. One day, with a lunch of peanut butter crackers and jars of Kool-Aid, we Butts Hollow boys climbed the hill behind the hollow until we came to the twisted wire cable that had somehow pulled free from the ground and dangled at an awkward angle from the telephone pole it was meant to brace. Before any of us could eat lunch, we had to swing out over the hollow on the cable. I was the last to go. I wasn't sure I wanted to, but I saw there was no choice. The other guys pushed me hard, and I flew out. It seemed like I was up over a mile. The empty lot where we played our football and baseball looked like a green postage stamp down below. What had seemed so big was, for a few seconds, all within my compass; I felt like I owned it.

Shot full of sudden exhilaration, I was ready to go again when the old lady whose property we were on came out of her house and started yelling at us. We ran for a while, and then slowed to a walk when we thought we were a safe distance away. Mike McKinney started making up a song about a mean old lady, but I didn't sing along. For days afterward, I skulked around waiting for something to happen—for the town cop to come to our door, for the old lady to stamp into our store and tell my parents. I was scared, and I knew it, and I didn't know that Mike's singing was all bluster.

I didn't like to fight; I didn't even like to get into arguments. I was an absentminded, dreamy kid. One of the older guys on the Midget football team started calling me Marilyn, after Marilyn Monroe, because while waiting for the coach to show up, I had a habit of lounging on the ball field, leaning on one outstretched arm with a sweet blade of grass in my mouth. Without knowing any better, I had affected the pose of a pinup girl. All the way into the fourth grade and I hadn't learned how to act like a boy or, worse, how not to act like a girl.

How was a boy to know? When the fire whistle sounded, my dad left the butcher shop in the rear of the store at a fast walk. Unknotting the string on his apron and leaving it on the checkout counter as he passed, he strode out into the street and stepped aboard the roaring fire engine as it shot by. Other men stepped from other stores and offices and did the same. On all their faces were set grins of anticipation. What was it they knew?

When Hemingway's Francis Macomber stands in to face the charging water buffalo and is wonderstruck by his moment of courage, Wilson, the white hunter, with British understatement, advises him, "Best not to talk about it." But how else to know?

When I started playing Midget football in the fourth grade, I was probably the youngest boy on the team. I did not understand football, did not understand offensive plays or defensive alignments. What I understood was that it looked beautiful out there under the lights at night, beautiful. Even when our side's uniforms were well worn and mismatched, I saw that the long runs down the sideline when a halfback threw his head back and kicked his legs and the defenders trailed him like the tail of a comet were wondrous and enviable and to be emulated, if I could only figure out how.

Sometime during my first-grade year, my dad had said, "Every day when you come home, run up that hill," meaning the steep hundred-or-so-yard hill up to our house.

"Why?" I asked him.

He looked a little baffled and looked away. *He didn't know, either,* I thought. Long years later I realized he thought his reason should have been all too obvious. Football practice was hard, the hardest thing I'd ever done, even if I got to participate in only a limited part of it. Every day we began by running four laps around the field, an impossible distance. The kids in the front jogged along and talked with what seemed to be little effort, while those of us in the back scrambled to keep up, cut corners when the coach wasn't looking. Then we did exercises: hundreds of jumping jacks, dozens of sit-ups and push-ups. We duck-walked up and down the field. At the command "Six inches!" from the boy who led us, we held our legs straight out barely above the ground. "Beat it out!" he would shout, and we would all pound our bellies with our balled-up fists. Then, for the rest of practice, all we littlest kids did was watch, moon around looking at the clouds, find the sweetest stems of grass and suck on them for moisture. At the end, I ran sprints with the rest of the team, and more laps. That practice was hard surprised me. Shouldn't beauty and grace come effortlessly? It looked that way to me.

Even that small bit of practice was enough. I had neither strength nor stamina, and both would be slow in coming. I was not designed to be an athlete, but that was the only way I saw to make myself into a grown man—that is to say, to avail myself of courage and to prove in some way that I had it.

At the high school, Coach Tommy Lucas believed in bravery, expected bravery. Maybe he even thought bravery could be taught. I was scared of him; I didn't know of any honest eighth or ninth grader who wasn't. On the first day of school, if the weather was fine, he would take the boys' physical education classes up onto the ball field and set them in the bleachers. He'd make a short speech about dressing for class on time and taking your gym clothes home and washing them at least once a week, about showering after class. And then he would walk off, leaving the class in the bleachers for the rest of the period, calling over his shoulder as he went, "Now, don't hurt anybody too bad." Then the upperclassmen formed two lines down on the field, and the eighth graders ran between the lines. Some juniors and seniors had fashioned special belts to wear on the first few days of school. Some were long enough to go around their owners' waists twice, others had holes punched in them, others had big brass buckles. At least the eighth-grade boys had on their street clothes and, if they were lucky or had foreseen this moment, had worn blue jeans to school that day. There was never a choice not to run. I never knew any boy who refused to take this initiation into high school. There would have been hell to pay for months and years if he had.

In the old schoolhouse on the hill, Coach Lucas had a game for cold or rainy days, when the boys had the gym. He had the class number off: one, two, one, two, fifteen to twenty boys on a side. Each side formed a line under a basket. In the middle of the court was a single basketball. When Lucas blew the whistle, everybody ran to the center for the ball. The object was to get hold of it and score a basket in any way you could. Boys lost track of their teammates in a wild scramble for the ball; they lost track of the idea of teams. A boy became his own one-man team. Punching, pinching, tripping, pushing—anything was allowed. If anybody hung back on the edge of this teeming scrum, Lucas was on the periphery with a broom to knock him back in there.

Were these ways of being brave?

Pocahontas was a coal camp, a town that had once boasted twenty-six saloons to serve three thousand people, a town that had once had its own distillery right on Center Street. One cold night, a man bought a little cask of whiskey from a bartender before head-ing home. Partway there, he tapped the keg and found it frozen inside. He turned his mule around and went back to town, walked into the bar, and shot the bartender without taking the trouble to ask for his money back first. As a girl, my mom once saw a man shot in the street. When she ran up the stairs with the news to the family's apartment over a store, her brothers could not be made interested enough to go see. It'd happened too many times before.

My parents remembered going to school with boys who'd beaten up teachers. Even so, in a town of hillbilly and immigrant coal miners, school was a civilizing influence. All my high school years, Gaza Kovach was the principal. He was made from the mold of an Old Country Hungarian peasant: very nearly square, big shouldered, thick necked, with short, stout arms and stubby fingers. He had been a football player in high school and college, a guard. But he had cherished ambitions to be a doctor until World War II interrupted his studies, and so he became a demanding and formidable teacher of physics and chemistry. Like Tommy Lucas, Gaza Kovach was somebody a boy was smart to be afraid of.

Each was a hard, physical man. Just for fun, Lucas would grab hold of a boy in the dressing room, wrap one strong arm around him, and give him a knuckle rub with the other. Or he might unexpectedly wrestle a kid to the floor and get the kid's arm in a half nelson. Gaza was known to grab hold of two boys at a time by taking their heads in the crooks of his arms and lifting them off the ground. "How you boys doing?" he'd shout. This was how we knew these men liked us.

Here is the complicated part, the part I believe Tommy Lucas and Gaza Kovach both understood but may never have articulated to each other or even to themselves. On the first day of school, Gaza gave his speech threatening bustings with boards for all offenses against school rules, most especially hazing. By the time you were a senior, you'd heard it five times. Later that same day, Tommy Lucas would walk off the ball field and leave thirty boys to "not hurt anybody too bad."

In his freshman year, David Kovach, the principal's son, got his nose broken by an upperclassman who cuffed him across the face. Maybe David was acting uppity for a freshman, maybe the upperclassman wanted to get in a lick on the principal's son, maybe he was doing what any upperclassman would do to any freshman given the chance. When David got home and his dad asked what had happened, David told him he'd run into a door. "You going to tell me who did that?" his father asked. No was the only possible answer, really. Every freshman boy knew this, and Gaza Kovach knew it, too.

Lucas and Gaza Kovach were preparing us boys for the world they had grown up in, the one they expected us to grow into. Most likely there were boys in our school who'd never been touched by their fathers at all except in anger. For them, the rough love at the hands of their principal and coach was as good as it got. And the undercurrent of rough behavior these men tolerated prepared us all for a world where we would most likely need to define ourselves in physical terms. Many of us would be coal miners, or leave the coalfields to find factory work, or join a branch of the armed services. Whether by accident or by design, their mixed messages taught us skills they believed we needed to survive.

To a lesser degree, my parents believed the same things as Gaza and Lucas. "When somebody hits you, hit 'em back," my mother told my brother and me. She grew up the only girl in a house of four brothers. Her mother died when she was twelve. "If they're bigger than you, hit them with anything you have." A baseball bat, a stick, a rock.

School was full of boys possessed of free-ranging anger. Homer Williby, who sat behind me in homeroom, had gray eyes with pupils like pinpricks. The homeroom teacher stood up in front of the room one afternoon and said, "I wish you all could have heard the presentation Frank Soos made in English class today." Homer grabbed hold of the back of my shirt. "I would have laughed and laughed," he told me, but his voice didn't sound like he'd ever laughed in his life. He played football and played a year of basketball but never went back out for the team. Really what he was best at was meanness. He is a guy I wonder about from time to time, wonder if he finally wore himself out on anger or went on to be a psycho killer, shooting people because he didn't like their haircuts or the color of the shirt they had on.

In a picture of the Varsity Club from the 1958 Pocahontas High School yearbook, *The Wigwam*, all the stars of the District VII championship basketball team are there, that team defined by grit and hustle—and courage, too, I'd say. None is taller than six feet. But standing among them is Jack Bradner, about six-three or -four. He had quit school years before and joined the army. After his hitch, he went back to finish school but was not allowed to play ball.

As we look at that picture in his old yearbook, Jack Richard McGinnis, one of the undersize forwards on that team, says, "We were boys; he was a man." When he graduated, Jack Bradner returned to the army and was among the earliest casualties of the war in Vietnam, killed by friendly fire. Looking at the picture a while longer, McGinnis says, "If he hadn't died in Vietnam, somebody would have killed him in the street."

Homer writes in *The Iliad* of warriors for whom "war itself became / lovelier than return, lovelier than sailing / in the decked ships to their own native land." That must have been how it went for Jack Bradner, who loved nothing better than to go among the beer joints in Pocahontas or Bluefield, drinking and mouthing until he picked a fight. Then, according to those who knew him, he didn't care if it was one man or two or three. He just had to fight them.

Jack Bradner may have been the model for a certain kind of Pocahontas ball player, a berserker. Certainly, his brother Gary could play only if he stretched himself to the outermost emotional edge. On the court, he was always one step away from saying something, something that might lead to a punch being thrown. His teammate Ray Hypes, gentle, mellowed from his own hard edge, says, "Hey, that was Gary; he had to play that way." As did those who followed in his mold—Harrell Erwin, Robert Howell, William Johnson.

For me, a basketball game was about beauty and ritual. But at some point it had to be about bravery, too. A ball game, even a basketball game, then seen as much more of a "noncontact" sport, is a little war. It has strategies, it has tactics. And while nobody wants a player to get hurt in a profound and lasting way, small hurts are expected and often part of a tactical decision, anything to take a hot player out of his game, to confuse him, to intimidate him. Rough him up a little, if that's what it takes to break his concentration.

Like Henry Fleming in Stephen Crane's novel *The Red Badge of Courage*, like Hemingway's Francis Macomber, these boys— because as Jack Richard McGinnis rightly said, we were all boys in our high-school selves—seemed to come to their fearlessness independent of conscious thought. And did they need to? And why would it be this self rather than a more gentle self they slipped into?

You might call the world of *The Iliad* prepsychological. It is a world ruled by petty jealousy, rage, revenge, and recrimination. The gods are your friends until they suddenly turn on you. Your allies are your friends, but sometimes they are weak-willed and fearful. The trouble is, nobody knows when or how a whole army of men will give up fighting. On one day the Greeks are fearless, relentless. They chase the Trojans back to their city gates and might destroy the city, but the time is not right, the fated actions are not in place. On other days, Trojans have all the courage; the Greeks flee to their ships. Yet these two contending armies have been at it for ten years. Like cross-county rivals, they know each other by name, by armor, by behavior. It's themselves they don't fully understand, how they can be fierce one day and frightened the next. Some god, maybe, has messed with their heads. But really they are struggling to know in just the same way any boy comes to wonder about his own performance on a ball court. How is it that one night you have a kind of radar for homing in on the basket, everything you shoot falls; when a ball goes up, you instinctively move to the right spot for a rebound; and when a player on the other team makes a pass, you step into the passing lane and steal it? But on another night, you are out of phase with your teammates and yourself; no matter what the stakes you cannot do what's asked of you.

Here's how it worked for me: My junior year, we were playing Northfork-Elkhorn a close game in our own gym. They'd beaten us easily down there. They were tough guys, and they came to play and expected to win. I was simply not in the game; as was often the case, I was off somewhere else, out of sync with my teammates and with the game. The coach took me out and made me sit on the bench and watch the guy who'd replaced me being knocked around. It made me mad to see him getting treated that way. I wanted back in and when I went in, I played aggressively and rough. We were doing better than holding our own when my teammate William lost his temper and started a fight with a Northfork player. That boy had lots of brothers and cousins, and they all stood up at once and started down from the bleachers to help him out. Our principal came out on the floor and sent them back up; the referees put both players out of the game. Whatever fire had been in my belly went out. We played on and took our beating.

Or sometimes like this: Once at Whitewood, before a packed gym, I played a good basketball game. I mean to say I played well by anybody's standards. For some reason that night I found my way into a frame of mind where I saw nothing but the ball and the other players, and wherever they were on offense, I was there to stop them. When a ball came off the backboard at our end of the court, I was right there waiting for it. In fact, I was often in the air waiting as the ball came off the rim. Still on my way up, I cradled the ball and dunked it over and in. In those days, a dunk was only offensive goaltending, and the basket was disallowed. From their seats right at goal level, the Whitewood fans could see my hand above the rim and inside the invisible cylinder that extended above it. Every time I stuck a rebound back over the lip of the basket, they howled. Yet my frame of mind was such that every angry shout seemed a little funny. I could not wipe the smirk off my face.

Courage in sport is defined in physical and often in violent acts. In the grown-up lives most of us live, the physical is removed and I hope the craving for violence is likewise. So I have to wonder, What good has all this ball playing done? What, if anything, useful has been learned? I am thinking of some very different Pocahontas ball players, who maybe learned the lessons they needed most playing football or basketball or both for Tommy Lucas.

When I see Robert Farley approaching the classroom building where we've agreed to meet and talk, I see his forward lean, his hands curled almost to fists. He walks a little on his toes as if always prepared to meet resistance, as if at any minute somebody might want to take a swing at him. He looks like the lunging bulldog on the hood of a Mack truck. Whatever may come, he wants to be ready.

Maybe Farley was the last man off the bench on the basketball team of 1965, the team that got within hollering distance of a state title. And by his own account, he was better at football. But he remains among the truest adult acolytes to Tommy Lucas, a man he admired and yet at the same time often hated. Basketball practice for Farley was boring, and he spent his time thinking he could coach the team better himself. His great ambition, a fantasy he nursed even as he was running laps at the back of the pack in the Pocahontas High School gym, was to go to college, get his degree, and get into coaching himself. He would find a job at a nearby school and come back and beat Tommy Lucas on his own floor.

Yet for all that, he grew into a man that Tommy Lucas both made and let him be. He tells me a story about an away game against Tazewell. When the game gets out of hand, Lucas tells his boys, "All right, take their names down. They have to come to our place and play." When they did, we would get them back. In the Lucas world, no slight could go unanswered. It was a lesson Robert Farley absorbed quickly. As a football player Farley would one day at practice tackle the assistant football coach who was quarterbacking the scrub team in his sweats. By stepping onto the field and running the plays, the coach had asked to be treated like a player. When he got tackled, he got what he deserved. The assistant insisted on a punishment and when Farley refused, he put him off the team. Lucas, the head football coach, overruled his assistant and let Farley back on. There was something about Farley's brashness, his willingness to take on anybody that Lucas valued, that he seemed to feel every team needed.

Meanness is not a skill in itself, but maybe a trait, and maybe Tommy Lucas thought it too could be taught, and maybe he thought it should be. It was a quality a guy wanted to shine off him when he went up to the Bluefield Auditorium or Mitchell Stadium and walked around in his letterman's jacket. It was what gave him the bravado he needed to go into a joint called the Sky Club, where fights were just another part of the night's entertainment. Farley believes he learned that sheen of meanness from Tommy Lucas. "Tommy took no captives," he says. Tommy Lucas was Farley's stick man when he walked out into the world, a kind of alter ego he would always be modeling himself on and measuring himself against.

I had no meanness. I knew it in my bones when I let myself slide so easily out of football. I had a ready-made excuse and I used it when guys asked me, but not many did. The summer before my sophomore year in high school, my mom told me I would have to get my weight up to 185 pounds if I expected to play football. I worked at it, eating bacon and eggs and drinking a quart of milk with Carnation Instant Breakfast powder every morning, eating and eating throughout the day. I would grow to six-three before the year was out, but I could not get my weight above 145. Freshman year, I'd been hurt on and off all season; but I let myself be hurt, I wallowed in my petty injuries. The game had taken a fiercer turn. It wasn't like Midget football where boys piled on each other like puppies. If football had ever been fun, it wasn't anymore. I wasn't sorry not to be out of there; nobody else cared. They weren't missing me.

Robert Farley is the father of two profoundly deaf sons, both educated in the public schools of Albemarle County, Virginia. It was a fight to get the county to come through; the Farleys fought them all the way on it. Robert Farley was argumentative, contentious, and litigious until he got the county to see things his way. As a result, he teaches in Midlothian County just north of Richmond, a hard hour-plus commute. He is sure he was blackballed by both the Albemarle County and Charlottesville City school districts because of his reputation as a troublemaker.

It is hard not to admire him. It is hard not to see his life as one continuation from the days when he tackled the assistant coach on the football field, when he fought one of his teammates in the locker room before the bus left for an away game. He snuck home and changed his torn shirt before Lucas could notice. Or a day much later when he had his college education and came down out of the bleachers along with his brother John to stand up for his youngest brother Dave in a fight with a ball player from Whitewood. That player had brothers and cousins, too. Again, Gaza Kovach made them all sit down.

Porter Murphy says, "I was mean. You have to be mean to play this game." He means basketball, not football, since for a brief time when he was in high school Pocahontas had no team. I think what he calls mean is something closer to focused determination.

After my own senior year in high school, I played some ball with Porter Murphy at the old schoolhouse up on the hill. It turns out I remembered him as much taller than he is, thinking of him as six-one, maybe even six-three, when he is really about five-eleven. His hands had seemed to me huge when spread across the belly of the ball, controlling it with such ease when he dribbled and when he shot. When we talked, he held his hand against mine and there I saw how small and even delicate it appeared compared with my own. I had studied him in 1968, his way of cutting from the wing in to the post—with or without the ball—and making a little jump hook from the center of the lane. I studied his shot choices, his clever passes. I studied his presence. Because despite my great height advantage and long, flailing arms when I came swooping in to try to block his shot, I could never get a hand on it. And then I would find he'd slipped around me somehow and had the inside position for a rebound.

In his way, the adult Porter was fearless as a matter of course. By then he had been in the air force, by then he had played on intramural teams on base when he was sometimes the only white player, played with and against guys taller and stronger than almost any he had seen in high school. What he called meanness I understood as not backing down, never being intimidated. Maybe his fearlessness came from knowing that if things came to blows, he would respond. I don't know. It never seemed to get that far with Porter or any of the Murphy brothers.

Gaza Kovach, Tommy Lucas, my parents grew up in the Depression and lived through World War II. Life, they would tell you, could not be lived if you let people push you around.

I didn't want to be pushed around, but I did not want to fight, either. I remember a fight, or what passed for a fight, between me and Larry Butt down in the vacant lot we called Butts' lot. He and I were about the same age, fourth graders I'd guess; he was small, wiry, surprisingly strong. He got me down and was on top of me. Would I give? he wanted to know. No, I told him, I wouldn't give. But I did not want to hit him, and he could not pummel me enough to make me give. Gradually, we both came to an understanding, that even if he made me say, "I give," I wouldn't mean it; I would just be saying it. There was no way he could use physical force to make me change my mind. Maybe if he had been meaner, maybe if I had more to fear.

In some important way, that was who I became, the guy you could get down on the ground, the one you could hurt some but who would not give. Throughout my boyhood I got into scrapes, apple battles with hard green crabapples (and every now and then a really rotten one just for a change), snowball fights, BB gun battles where I was truly fodder, never being allowed to own a BB gun. But I stayed away from real trouble; I went the long way around any situation that might turn into a fight with fists.

Being a boy who would not give wasn't enough, though, was it? That same fourth-grade year, a big fire burned almost a block of Center Street: Mustard's dry goods store, the Palace movie house, a dry cleaner, and the Methodist church. The fire was fearful and it was inspiring. As my friend Alfred and I watched from the sidewalk in front of my parents' store, high-school boys in their varsity jackets ran into the burning church, ripped the pews from the sanctuary floor, and dragged them outside. They saved the pulpit, the pulpit Bible, the heavy wooden chairs with their red velvet cushions the preachers sat on, the baptismal font, the altar table, and, most important of all, the heavy golden cross that sat on it. Then the fire punched through the tin roof and the sanctuary collapsed.

What I can tell you now is that those boys weren't Methodists or particularly religious at all. They had been caught up in a kind of romance that made it impossible to resist rushing into the burning church and saving its symbols. Nobody ran into the movie house or dry goods store. When it was time, Alfred and I went on to school, as did most of the high-school boys. But the fire burned all day, and my dad and all the other volunteer firemen from Pocahontas, Bramwell, and Graham fought it. They suffered from minor burns and smoke inhalation. They got up the next morning and went back to their jobs. I wondered if when the time came I would have the courage to rush into a burning building and make myself a hero.

The Iliad and *The Odyssey* were no help to me here. In the children's versions I read as a boy, war as rendered by Jane Werner Watson was not hell but a beautiful game. Here's a sample of the stuff I read: "Thus Hector, son of Priam, like the war god himself spurred the Trojans on. And he flung himself into the battle like a whirlwind from the upper air sweeping down on the sea. Who fell first and last to the mighty Hector? There were too many to name." Such words. And coupled with illustrations of warriors in their horsehair helmets, with their spears and shields. Menelaus and Paris square off in stances familiar to any ball player in any sport, knees flexed, weight over the balls of their feet, bodies leaning forward. Take away their weapons and they would look like point guards or linebackers.

What Watson's stories did not clue me in to and what Homer does not stint on are the attendant horrors of war. Men rarely go down to death expeditiously. In his rage after the death of Patroclus, Achilles comes upon an unarmed son of Priam:

> At this the young man's knees failed, and his heart;
> he lost his grip upon Achilles' spear
> and sank down, opening his arms. Achilles
> drew his sword and thrust between his neck
> and collarbone, so the two-edged blade went in
> up to the hilt. Now face down on the ground
> he lay stretched out, as dark blood flowed from him,
> soaking the earth. Achilles picked him up
> by one foot, wheeled, and slung him in the river
> to be swept off downstream.
>   (*The Iliad*, book 21, lines 119–128)

War is cruel and unfair, and there are no referees. Maybe I needed Homer to teach me this. Despite the rough-and-tumble world of coal camps where my high-school basketball was mostly played, despite the fights and technical fouls, the basketball we played was surprisingly clean. Gratuitous elbows were rare. Maybe because games were called so closely, players had no fouls to spare. I was always in foul trouble and remain convinced I didn't commit most of them. Still, even when I disagreed with the refs' calls, I thought they were my friends. In the most hostile gyms, I always believed the referees would insulate me from the fans—at least as long as the game was under way.

Basketball, no matter how poorly I played it, no matter how rough any game might be, was no kind of model of how the world worked. On our TV, getting harder and harder to ignore, the war in Vietnam was raging. Some of those players who graduated ahead of me, those same guys who saw the service as their ticket out of the coal mines, were "in country."

Meanwhile, I tried odd cerebral experiments in courage. In a college intramural game, I threw an elbow into the chest of the guy guarding me, an end on the football team who could have broken me in two if he chose to. He was baffled and angry. Another time, I pointed out the guy I was picking up man-to-man—"the fat one," I said in a voice that carried across the court. What was I trying to prove, anyway? I don't know except there are now these guys out in the world who are justified in thinking I'm an ass.

In Herb Francisco's house, in a prominent place in his living room, is a pen-and-ink drawing of a dog—the dog that saved his life. Herb, one of those players who wound up drafted into the army, was walking point with his dog on a patrol when they were ambushed. The other men in his squad were killed, and Herb lived because the Vietcong who examined him saw the blood from his dead dog sprayed all over him and decided Herb had to be dead, too. Herb lay there holding his breath—as ants walked across his face, as the soldier stood above him and considered whether to put an insurance round in him—and did not move.

This would be the Herb Francisco Tommy Lucas called the most natural athlete he'd coached. This would be the Herb who threw himself so fully into his ball games that he ended up in the emergency room more than once. And this would be the Herb whose practical jokes could stray over the line into the cruel. This would be the Herb who comes from a family of men who develop heart trouble young, whose dad died when he was four. As a result he believes Lucas took a special interest in him. Herb had open-heart surgery at an age when most of us are still playing city-league ball. And he has been married and divorced three times. "You could blame it on Vietnam, but that would be wrong."

When I talk to Herb, he is babysitting one of his grandchildren—a surprisingly strict grandpa. As with Robert Farley, I find myself admiring the man Herb has become: wiser, calmer, a guy who can admit his mistakes and maintain his dignity. Is this what happens to a man when a rifle plays over him and he waits for a fate he cannot control?

When I came home during my sophomore year in college, my hair had grown down to my shoulders. My dad told me to go up the street and get it cut. I started off for the barbershop and then turned back. "Are you going to get it cut?" he said. No, I told him. He growled, but turned away. He let it go, probably the first time I had disobeyed him. Maybe it was about time.

That same year, I would go to my first anti-war march. One afternoon, my friend Mark and I drove in to Charlotte in his roommate's car to meet the people who were organizing the march. In addition to the college-age and slightly post-college-age, there were the true organizers, a group of Quaker men, men my father's age. I realized these men had resisted World War II; they weren't just against the war in Vietnam, they were against every war. The day of the march, there were few of us, maybe a hundred or so. We assembled at the downtown Charlotte post office and walked up to the intersection of Trade and Tryon streets. The route was lined by jeering patriots—I guess that's what they would have called themselves—and by cops. One cop had a movie camera and another a still camera, and they did their best to make sure they got a picture of each of us. I carried no sign, just walked along with my hands jammed in the pockets of my barn coat.

What, I wonder, would Tommy Lucas have thought of my doings on that day? Was this being brave when guys like Diz and Benny Murphy hunkered down under the Tet Offensive, when Herb lay under the gun barrel? Was it an act that might in some way be a continuation of my initiation into high school, of running laps and doing push-ups and leg lifts, of standing in to take a charge?

Because I had never played for Lucas, because I could never know what it felt like to withstand his hardest practices of full-court drill after full-court drill, to stand up to his withering belittlements, to meet his demands simply to play better, I could never know. Part of me wanted some certification of bravery. I thought if you won ball games you must have some skills, but at some point some courage as well. There comes a moment in almost every ball game when you win because you want to win more than the other team. The teams I played on didn't win many games.

A few years ago I went to a Little League baseball game with a friend of mine. His kid, while playing third base, had fallen into a reverie and had taken off his glove, and he was moving it through the soft summer air as if it were an airplane or space ship. I could remember myself having this kind of moment and then some. I want to believe that one of the things Tommy Lucas was good at was busting such nonsense right out of a boy, of getting and keeping his attention. What do we call that state, that state where mere adolescent ego is torn away and nothing is left but a ball, the basket, and expectations? What if a boy comes up to those expectations? Is it right to call that courage?

After spending six months in the hospital recovering from lung cancer and its attendant complications, my father was released to go home. During that time, he had grown too weak to walk and had to learn all over again. Because my parents' house had only one bathroom, on the second floor, he had to demonstrate he could climb a flight of stairs before he could be released. Together he and I practiced the thirteen steps in the hospital stairwell until he mastered them. On the drive home he said, "As soon as we get there, I'm going to walk up those steps and hug your momma's neck." And he did, this man who never ran a lap or played a game of Tommy Lucas basketball.

One day late in winter, what we sometimes call spring in Alaska, I was skiing a fifty-kilometer ski marathon. The air was cold and so was the snow, making the skating technique I'd chosen more than difficult. Before I had skied half the course, I was struggling. But my wife-to-be and my truck were waiting at the finish, so there wasn't much to do but go on. With ten kilometers to go, both my hamstrings began to cramp. I was able to double-pole along for a few hundred meters and then ski for a few hundred, and in this way I came to the finish with enough energy left to scramble up the riverbank and into a warm building. I was done; but what, truly, had I accomplished?

The day of the anti-war march, I just walked and let my picture be taken. It was an act that stood outside vanity or shame. Looking back, I think maybe it was a brave act; maybe it was a start toward what courage might really be.

Now I am fifty-six. I have taught on various levels for more than thirty years, yet if I died tomorrow I think I would have spent more time in gyms and locker rooms, on ski and running trails, and on handball courts than I ever have in a library or at my desk practicing the craft of writing.

Though I've never been particularly good at any of the sports I've tried to play, I did play and continue to do so because I believed as a boy that sport was beautiful and glamorous. I believed as a young man that it would build my character. While I haven't abandoned those notions, I now sometimes think that if there were a sport that did not require speed, grace, or strength, one that was determined by simply refusing to give up, then I might be good at such a sport. But who would know how to measure or judge such a thing? And what would you call it?

Obituary with Bamboo Fly Rod

Here's a story Dave Stark told me: Once he and another guy from Fairbanks drove over Murphy Dome to do some fishing on the lower Chatanika. On the west side of the dome, the road drops down into a permafrost bog. That's where they got balled up in the mud on that one-lane road too skinny to turn around on. Equipped with nothing but an ax and a come-along, they spent the better part of an Alaskan summer day pulling themselves out of the muck and yanking the truck around in the road for the trip back over the dome. I'm not sure they did any fishing at all.

I used to teach high-school English in a little town in piedmont North Carolina, a little town that lies along the road from the Charlotte airport to my parents' home in Virginia. There, in my very first year of teaching, I taught a boy who was clearly smarter than I was, than I would ever hope to be. I saw his quickness instantly, the way he probed a short story and came out with things, made connections that none of the other kids quite saw, that I saw but had to admit I wouldn't have thought of myself. Because I was a new teacher, I didn't have the self-assurance, the presence of mind to see that at least I had the edge in simple knowledge. I taught this young man for three years, coached him in cross-country, led him on hikes with the outing club. When I moved on to graduate school, I started a short list, the kind of list I wonder if all teachers don't secretly keep, of the truly gifted, of those marked for some future distinction. For a few years, he remained the only one on that list. And I waited for his name to turn up in the newspaper, maybe in the book reviews or academic journals. I was sure it would turn up somewhere so that even way over in Alaska, I would detect the ripple.

That's the kind of information I'm on the lookout for when I read the paper, the little connections that assure me that through a messy web of tangles the world is held together. Everybody scans the paper for the big stuff, who's bombing whom, further proof of what scoundrels we've elected to high office; but I want to get around that to the revelations of the human heart also to be found right there in the daily newspaper. For this reason I must read both Dear Abby and Ann Landers, along with the features on outstanding local schoolchildren; the sports page with particular emphasis on the compiled statistics of hometown leagues and results of local foot, dog sled, and automobile races; the announcements of engagements, weddings, and births; the letters to the editor; and the court judgments and police blotter.

There in the police blotter, on a dark day deep in the bottom of winter, among the requisite petty thieveries, DWIs, and collisions, I saw a report of a man found dead in his apartment, dead of a gunshot wound. Foul play was not suspected, but I wasn't mystified. I know how to read the mildly evasive language of the police report.

I know the spot on the lower Chatanika Dave Stark was headed for. I know the road up the Fairbanks side of Murphy Dome. That road leads to my house, but to get to the river you'd go past my turn and on up the dome. Toward the top, the road flattens out and you can see you're pretty much above the tree line and into tundra. Some willow shoots line the road, but behind them are big patches of blueberries and low bush cranberries. In the late summer, we go there to pick those berries, especially in the fields just below the air force radar installation. And if that place is too crowded or overpicked, we will go out the road onto the saddle below the dome. From there, the road drops off toward the Chatanika River and Minto Flats beyond. Which is why, they say, this road to almost nowhere exists. A state senator wanted a quicker way to get out to the flats for his bird hunting, his moose hunting, his pike fishing than driving all the way around to the far side, to the new Minto Village off the Elliott Highway.

This state was rich then. Putting a rough road through with a couple of Caterpillar tractors and a heavy road grader so a senator and his buddies could more conveniently slip away to the real Alaska was no big deal. Alaska isn't so rich now, and that senator is dead. The road has deteriorated. I wouldn't try it except in a truck with four-wheel drive. I always remember to carry a come-along and an ax, too.

I found the rest of the story of the dead man a few days later when I read another part of the paper I read daily without fail, the obituaries. A modern obituary is often a stingy bit of reportage; nobody wants to get too close to revealing a cause of their grief. This one was more forthcoming than most. The dead man was older than I was, though not by much. He would have been a senior in high school when I was a freshman, one of the big guys who punched freshmen in the arm, smoked behind the gym, had a girl and his own car spotted with primer. And he was one who wound up in Vietnam, regardless of whether he intended to.

It might be too easy to imagine that nothing went right from there. He had a string of jobs, was a policeman in two states, sold cars and was good at it, mined gold, worked for the Bureau of Land Management. Left a couple of wives, a couple of kids in different states. Most recently, he lived with yet another woman. Maybe he gave up on the durability promised by a ceremony. And maybe at the end as he died of cancer, as death became more inevitable and life more painful, neither she nor anybody else could do anything to help him.

He owned, the obituary says, a bamboo fly rod, his grandfather's old rod, his grandfather from back in Missouri. I lived down in Arkansas for a while where the runoff from the fertilizer and chicken litter had ruined the fish for eating. So maybe I envied the people up in Missouri, where the water ran cold and clear out from the bottoms of hydroelectric dams and made the fishing for trout good year-round. I wondered how it was then, when his grandfather must have caught rainbows as long as your arm fishing the tailwaters down from the sluice gates. That would have been before the editors of fishing magazines started running feature stories, the kind where a fisherman in waders kneels before the camera offering up a subdued and weighty fish in his outstretched arms. And I wondered what it was like to come to own such a fine fishing rod, a rod that had some fishing in it, and I considered why, in the end, it wasn't enough.

Sometimes a thing comes into your hands without its history attached. Sometimes you have to figure it out by yourself. After it has been used awhile, a bamboo rod can take a set, a noticeable bend in the tip section of the rod. A casting set, its tip bending upward, is an indication of many more casts than fish taken, and a fighting set means a rod has taken its share of big fish, fish that took something out of the rod. My own bamboo rod arrived without a casting or a fighting set. It said very little of who had owned it except that perhaps one day he put it up wet and stored it carelessly. The steel guides rusted through their wraps, the varnish crazed.

Shouldn't it be otherwise? Shouldn't the elegant old thing come dragging the past behind it? When I am on the riverbank with my bamboo rod in hand, I want to stand in the present and look back into a past that leads not only inevitably to this moment, but to the rightness of this moment. Norman Maclean might think so, too. I've read in *A River Runs through It* where he says nobody ought to be allowed to catch a fish off a bad cast. To think such a thing is to believe in the rightness of nature, or in the case of Mr. Maclean, to believe in the complicity of God with nature, God lurking in the background to make sure things come right.

And I think, *What about accidents?* Accidents, for example, like the one where I overshoot my cast, and it flips up around a twig hanging over the river, swinging just a minute before it slithers off and into the water. A fish maybe has caught a glint off the hook and is rising to take the fly even as it falls. And I think if we're going to disallow that catch, then what about fish caught on poorly tied flies, caught on flies tied in Third World countries by underpaid peasants? Fish caught on cheap outfits that are an insult to the art of fishing, or fish caught on overpriced ones bought by the vainglorious who think a brand name says something about their human worth? If you took those reasons into account, who among us has caught many fish worth mentioning?

Among the stories I took up with my high-school students was Joseph Conrad's *Heart of Darkness*. It is not a particularly easy story to get to go in a high-school classroom. I found myself taking my students through it one sentence at a time in places, feeling a little like the narrator Marlow himself chugging up an unknown river—always against the current—in his steamer. It was a worthwhile trip for me if only because I taught myself something I'd managed never to see clearly in four years as an English major at a pretty good school. Here were great paragraphs. Here were paragraphs that ran sentences by the reader like rivers of words, sometimes rushing, sometimes majestic and barely seeming to move at all. Here was a skill you could spend your life trying to grab on to.

And my student, the smart one on my very short list, saw Conrad's genius, too, though he thought for a minute it might be me. "The man really knows how to read this stuff," he told a bunch of other kids as one class pushed out the door against the next one coming in. Still, I was relieved. I thought I had taught him something useful.

There is a need in all of us, I think, to believe the world is somehow ordered. In the river there are fish. Even if our eyes are good, we rarely see them, yet we cast into the pools at the spots where we expect them to be holding. The flies we use are often the flies we used the last time the light was like this, the water this high, the season right about now. Often this method works. We cast, and sure enough, just like last year, there's a fish rising, revealing itself.

One afternoon, driving my brother's car home to see the folks, I took the exit off the interstate, drove into town and up the main street divided by the little-used railroad tracks, took the right on Center Street, and parked in front of the school where I had taught. Maybe it was ten years, maybe fifteen. But everything was just as it had been, the same school secretary, my friend the physics teacher still in his same room, still at his desk grading some tests or lab reports. I sat down at a student desk and pretty soon many of the other teachers I had known came by. My ex-uncle-in-law was there, and so the talk turned to my other ex-in-laws and where they were and how they were doing. Which saddened and embarrassed me, to think that a whole part of my life had sheared off and drifted away from me like an iceberg. Rick came up, my ex brother in law, as smart and mulish a man as I've ever known. I believe I'd like him even still, though I bet he has gone Republican on me.

"He was our only Morehead Scholar," somebody said. And I said, no, my student had been a Morehead Scholar, too.

"You know what happened to him, don't you?"

"No." And I believe I wanted to know.

"He killed himself." Nobody knew why. That's too bad, we all said; that's a shame. But we were friends who hadn't seen each other in a long time, so our talk moved on.

It's hard not to blame myself. That's another secret list I suspect most teachers have, the list of all the mistakes you've made, all the things you could have done differently, said differently, or never said at all. It's one thing when the guy you sent to the principal's office once a week knocks over a gas station, it's another when it's a kid off your short list. Here was a kid with the world rolling out in front of him, just waiting for him to walk in it, to make a piece of it his own. What went wrong? And what could I have said or done that would have stopped it?

How to be? That's what Conrad really wants to know. That's what I sometimes worry that Norman Maclean wants to come at a little too easily, something having to do with his Presbyterianism. God is out there and has the whole thing planned out. Except there's the central problem of *A River Runs through It*, the wonderfully gifted brother, dead of another kind of self-destruction. Despite the rich, assuring language of Mr. Maclean's closing paragraphs—the river has cut through the rock as ordained for ages—the brother's death stands a senseless, unnecessary act. Death cannot be reconciled despite a wash of words. How, then, to be?

In the obituary before me, I read that our man has been awarded three Bronze Stars for valor and a Purple Heart. You'd think that would be lesson enough. You'd think that having steamed upriver with Marlow, my student would have seen the horror of a life unraveled. You'd think lessons learned at such young ages would wrap themselves around a person like a magic girdle, making these men somehow immune from failures at marriage, failures at work, accrued disappointments. If not immune from disease, then immune from the humiliation, the degradation of constant pain and physical decline.

At its tip, a well-made bamboo fly rod is about the diameter of the lead in a wooden pencil. Six sections of split, planed, and tapered cane have been fitted together so as to appear a single piece of wood. A picture of a good fisherman caught at the end of his backcast will show the butt of the rod upright and barely passing beyond the perpendicular line made by his body. But the upper section of the rod will be well bent, trailing behind with the line almost like an elongated pennant. Despite the great force brought to bear on it, as near as I can tell, such a rod can't really be worn out.

For a while, though, that's why I thought bamboo rods came with two tips, that somehow you could fish the life out of one. But it turns out this isn't so. Most bamboo rods get their tips snapped off in car doors, against tree trunks, under the feet of careless or clumsy fishermen.

One of the most satisfying experiences you can have as a teacher is for one of your old students to look you up. Just to say hello, just so you can see he's doing okay in this world. Jeff was such a guy. As a student, he'd been stubborn and absent-minded. A long-distance runner and cyclist with out-of-the-way interests for a high-school boy in cooking and sewing. Now he was a cowboy, a real one, and a farrier and a saddle maker. I took a look at the pictures of his leatherwork, the English and western saddles, and saw in the clean sure lines that he'd grown himself a sense of style. The saddles were elegant, functional things.

Our talk turned, as I knew it would, to my student on the short list and, of course, Jeff knew about the same facts I did. Maybe it was his job, maybe his marriage. We were back to saying another round of too-bads. Only this time we were eating Italian food in Alaska when it was twenty below outside. "He sure is missing a lot of fun," the cowboy said.

Well, yeah. We fly-fish in the pouring rain, ski in the freezing cold when anybody with sense would sit home by the fire. We invite pain and discomfort into our lives. And I guess I do it in part for practice. So that on the days when pain and discomfort come unbidden and won't go away, I will have somehow prepared myself.

I have no confidence this trick will work. If it did, the suasive powers of writers like Joseph Conrad and Norman Maclean would be enough to make us all look into our souls and come up better for it. We'd come to know badness for what it is and stay away from it. The fly-caster's four count beat would be a kind of mantra for us all, suggesting a mechanism for a life of precision and control. Our ethical behavior would grow naturally from the beauty of these writers' words.

It has been a few years since I've fished the lower Chatanika, the place where Dave Stark got bogged down. I've decided I don't much like to fish that spot. You come out on the river at a long, flat pool, a good place to launch a boat, but no use to a fisherman without one. Upriver is an island and on its west side is a deep hole promising all sorts of fish. I've tried it with dry fly, wet fly, nymph, and streamer but never taken a fish out of it. There are two hundred yards or so of good water just above that hole where big fish can be found in the late fall. And beyond that, more straight water where sometimes a fish or two can be had. But there are no compelling fishing problems here, no sweepers hanging over the river, no riffles to channel the current, no combination of tricky turns and rocky hiding places that make a spot a fishing revelation. And there is the road. That muddy track through permafrost looks to be a clean shot to the river as you approach it from the saddle above. But every year it makes itself more a pathless wood, a muddy bog that can leave you far from the river with no chance of turning back.

How to be? For that poor guy holding on to his grandpa's bamboo rod, full of bright promises of clear water and big fish, it somehow was not enough to preserve him. A mistake, maybe, to think the objects of this world have talismanic qualities. Having the old man's rod, we think we have his experience, his wisdom. Maybe we do if we look at it another way. The rod cannot say what wisdom grandpa had. It can only be a tool in your hand. You can fish with it through good days and bad. If you know how to find fish and know how to cast with it, the rod will help you catch them. You can use it, and maybe learn some things for yourself.

I take to the river in the last good days of fall. The leaves are yellow and dropping, but the river is still full of life. Bugs are rising, and the fish are following them to the surface. In the quiet, I cast and hear my line rattle through the guides as my own bug settles on the water. Soon, it will be cold; the fish will regard my flies from the river's bottom with lazy suspicion. Here are days; there won't be any others.

Upside-Down with
Borges and Bob

From here, I see my truck as a big red rock thrown into the lake of my life.

Thirty-five feet down the bank, its dusty entrails exposed to the sky, the driver's side door cocked open at an odd angle so the dome light casts a weak peach tint onto the snow, it looks worse than maybe it is. I see the bright silver casing of the newly overhauled transmission with less than a hundred shifts in it, the new front brake hoses; everything exposed to me looks to be in perfect working order, if only it were right-side up.

It is not. And no amount of wishing on my part will make it so. The wrecker is on its way; and while I wait I consider the ripples my rock has made. Things could have been worse, my wife tells me. I have to agree. One possible rippling wave out to the future does not contain me at all. Instead of standing on the shoulder assuring passing drivers that I am all right despite all indications I ought to be otherwise, I could be history, gone, out of here.

"Did your life flash before your eyes? Did you see any interesting sights?" my friend Farnham asks me a few days later. I saw my truck sliding up the road wildly to the right, and then, after some furious steering, sliding wildly to the left; I saw it headed back to the right again, and this time as the road curved to meet it, there was not enough space to execute any more desperate maneuvers. I say "I saw" because it seems to me now that I can actually see this wreck as if I were hovering above it in a helicopter, no longer a participant but a witness.

In his *Labyrinths*, Jorge Luis Borges suggests we can live thousands of parallel lives of the imagination—an idea that appeals to me just now. In one of these lives I am efficient, organized. In another I ski like an Olympic medalist. In another I am a fabulously successful writer. In another I have chosen a different route, a different time, a different kind of weather for myself. Not one of these alternative versions would have me standing by the roadside shivering and waiting on the wreck truck.

When I try these Borges premises on a class full of undergraduates, they have no trouble seeing it for the hooey it is. Who would trade in the life we are living for any imagined life, even if that imagined life contains no vehicles in the ditch, insurance adjusters, smart-aleck wreck truck drivers, leisure-prone auto body men? Nonetheless, I am still attracted to the idea of following myself along, being myself in two places at once. I am both driving the truck and watching myself, or watching the truck with me in it. And I feel compelled to run this film loop again and again. Here comes my truck down a slight incline. To the right hugging the shoulder is a kid on a snow machine (as we call snowmobiles around here). I say kid because I knew he was a kid before I ever saw him. I saw his snaky track playing into the road, crossing over into the left lane, making spins and squiggles for a couple of miles before I came upon him. Only a kid would play in the road this way. Not because adults don't play on their snow machines; they do all the time. That's what they're for. But an adult would have a truck and maybe even a trailer and pull his snow-go out to the nearby hills where you can play without worrying about the traffic. Somehow the kid hears my engine through his crash helmet and over the sound of his own engine and pulls well to the right so I can pass him.

I wave, and he waves back. At least I think we exchange these waves. And I think it partly because as I struggle to orient myself in the upside-down cab, it is the kid who is outside my window digging in the dirt trying to help me free the door. While nothing else quite makes sense—bottom is now top, left is now right—I know my rescuer is this high-school kid.

How did this happen? Sometime after I pass him, maybe a couple of hundred yards, on the uphill climb, accelerating to pick up the momentum I lost when I slowed to pass him, I begin sliding. Quickly enough, I come to a stop.

Inside my capsule, the light is dim. I can see nothing out the front; the windshield is shattered and pushed into the snowy ground. Around me are familiar objects in unfamiliar places, schoolbooks, my boots, a scattered mess of clothes that have escaped the unzipped gym bag that was on the seat beside me. An ax. It had been behind the seat, as had a heavy canvas bag of tools pulled out only yesterday to fix a broken spoke on my bicycle. I had meant to put it back.

At some point, at a time before the kid came to dig at the window, I punched the button on my seat belt and fell softly into the ceiling of the truck. It wasn't a long fall. I had already conducted an almost instant inventory of my own systems and had convinced myself I was okay. I had the sense to turn off the radio, which was running a feature about red wine and French cooking. The point of this feature seemed to be that if you ate all that rich food it would eventually kill you, regardless of how much red wine you took with it. I had suspected as much.

About this one thing, Borges is undeniably right. We are born and then, after a while, if we're lucky, we die. It's how we manage what's in the middle that matters. But unlike the characters we meet in his story "The Garden of the Forking Paths," I cannot accept with equanimity a future that excludes me. I cannot imagine a world without me in it. Even the rippling wave of possibility that runs on without me still contains my conscious presence. I imagine my wife grieving, and because she is strong, I imagine her surviving all right without me. She lies on the couch surrounded by her cats as always. Sadder. The cats pick up on this sadness and snuggle closer to comfort her. But after a while, she gets up; she eats, she prepares for her classes and even does the ugly work of taking up the loose ends of my own. But through seeing her act this way, I remain a constant presence. My wife's future life spools out of my head. I may imagine it one way this minute and another the next; maybe she is more angry at my foolishness than sad, more organized herself as a result of seeing me off with so much left undone. Maybe she uses the insurance money for handmade red and black cowboy boots. But it is still my imagination at work. And it is for this reason I literally cannot imagine a future that in some way does not contain me.

I had not expected to be hearing the news of death by French cooking quite this way. I always suspected something was going to kill me, too, maybe cancer, maybe heart failure, maybe an accident of one kind or another. But I had not believed it and still do not believe it. If I did, would I have spent the past few Sunday hours differently? Wouldn't I have started on a melodramatic made-for-TV quest for peace, love, or justice? Instead I had spent my time driving to school, talking to a few students, driving to Birch Hill and skiing, and while skiing thinking alternately about my form, particularly why it was so bad, and about politics, people, my upcoming sabbatical leave when I planned to put my life in order and get oodles of work done. Would I have driven to Fox to get some springwater for our coffee and tea? Would I have stopped halfway there to look in the bed of the truck for my thought-to-be-missing ski gloves?

Would I have spent the past almost forty-four years any differently at all? Would I still be waiting for my sabbatical to put my life in order? No and yes. Based on the evidence that is myself, what other honest conclusion could I draw?

My neighbor Bob Bell puts his hand up to the top of my head. "I just wanted to see if you were any shorter after your wreck." When I was driving, I could sense the presence of the roof less than an inch above my head, feel, when the weather was right, the pull of static electricity drawing my hair up to the roof liner. And to the left, also very near my head, was what car-crash people call the A-pillar, the part of the frame that supports the roof, that the doors nestle into. In collisions, it's common for people to get thrown against the A-pillar. Such a wreck usually doesn't kill you. But it mushes up the left side of the brain, the cell clusters that control language and speech. Hitting the A-pillar turns you into a noncommunicating idiot with a healthy appetite and a seventy-five-year life span.

I know this. I knew it all along. But only rarely have the proximity to my head of the roof liner and the A-pillar caused me to drive more slowly. Bob Bell tells me about a wreck he had driving a heavy dump truck at the gold mine where he works. The brakes failed on his first run of the day, and he went head over a fifteen-foot bank. "It was like an invisible hand held me back. First run of the day, I didn't even have my seat belt on." Somehow Bob didn't fly into his windshield. Inside his pickup, Bob's daughter reads a magazine by the dome light, oblivious. "It was a miracle. I believe in miracles."

I wish for miracles myself. And I wonder what constitutes a miracle these days. In Bob's case, he was unbruised, uncut. The speed of the brakeless truck threw his twenty tons of gravel out ahead of him when he hit the bank, cushioning the fall instead of rushing against the bed and crushing him. This is miracle enough for a man who believes in miracles.

And for the guy who doesn't? Bob's wreck was a model of Newtonian physics. I think of a little car we rolled across the lab table in my high-school physics class. Pull the pin with the attached string and a steel ball is launched mortar style out of the top of the car. Left alone, car and ball continue on their way until the ball falls back to earth and is caught—miraculously?—in the metal cup that launched it. Stop the car and the ball goes on without it. Stop Bob's truck as it tilts over the embankment and the gravel flies over the bed, passing the truck. Momentum.

Or loss of control. "I made a mistake," I tell Bob. "No," he says, "you had an accident." It's all a question of control. My own or somebody else's. When Bob ran over the bank in his dump truck, the faulty brakes were outside his control. Somebody in maintenance didn't do his job. And then God, or something very like God, stuck a big hand out and kept Bob Bell from slamming through the windshield of his truck.

"Going too fast, weren't you," the wrecker owner says, fixing me with his bloodshot eyes. He's seen it all; he knows. "Two-wheel or four-wheel?" I admit to him, "Two." He looks away. I am just too stupid for words. A slick road, fresh snow on top of a little ice, snow blowing and cutting down on visibility. Here I come in two-wheel drive like it's Sunday in July.

In Bob's view, a miracle might be the presence of God and the absence of control. God will take care of things in whatever way suits him. All of us agree with Bob on some level. If I go back in time, I see no need to alter my grandfather's failing health. To do so is only to postpone an understood inevitability. I can't stop his death from happening, only delay it. In this way, I accept for others what I cannot accept for myself. I fight against it like a fish against the surprising hook and line.

What if, as Borges suggests in "The Secret Miracle," time might come in bubbles like notes of music, given different values and filling up different durations? I slow my life to adagio. And I know for a fact I can make this happen, having traveled along the Blue Ridge Parkway at high speed, a classical recording in the tape deck that slowed the world through the windshield down to a majestic crawl. Within those notes, full and fat as grapes ready to burst their skins, I have rolled along well beyond the posted speed limit, believing in the power of my synapses to direct my feet properly to accelerator, clutch, and brake. And believing no deer, possum, or skunk would pick such a moment in time to saunter out of the laurel and onto the road. Nonsense and stuff. And a 360-degree spin in the wet road was enough—for a short time—to convince me. Despite neurons racing like lightning, my poor muscles and bones remained long and slow. The music is mere artifice, illusion. My momentum carried my truck right down the bank. The wheels being cocked to the right as the truck began its descent caused the truck to begin to lose its balance to the left. Slowly, slowly it began to roll over. I say "slowly" because although I couldn't keep up with the images flashing through the windshield—they were coming in too fast for me to see myself going over—I could tell what was happening. I could tell the struggle was over. Maybe I felt it in my inner ear. Maybe my brain really did process the images but didn't know how to tell me what it was seeing. Something like this must have happened: as I began to roll, my body relaxed. The inertia of the truck pulled it down while I leaned away from the fall, almost laying my head against the back of the seat. Then my head swung back straight. Only I was upside down. I knew this in the same way I knew I was unhurt. The power switch on the radio was exactly where it should have been, so I reached out and turned it off. Only then did everything stop making sense. Only then did I start trying to put words to it.

Let's just say I could stand on the roadside and make a hole in time, a tear in the cloth, and crawl through it, into it. Wouldn't I do everything differently this time? I would not, for example, sleep through almost all of my eight o'clock classes as a college freshman, through many of my nine o'clock ones as a sophomore and junior. I would sit in front of that brown calculus book and fight with stolid courage until I got it, until integrals and derivatives actually meant something real to me. I would not waste electives on sociology; I would go to the May Day anti-war rally and put myself in the road, stop traffic on the bridges from northern Virginia to DC. Maybe I would even ask that redheaded woman who went to Queens College for a date and not look at my shoes. In short, I would be smarter and better and more self-assured.

What about my wife? To change the past is to change the present, too. And what is that ache to return all about, but to go back and take a kink or two out of time? Maybe not fix the little goofs—never getting to the end of *The Pickwick Papers* or *Humphry Clinker*—but taking corrective actions against the biggies. Get rid of my first marriage. But if it weren't for the pitiful mistakes of the first, how would I ever have had enough sense to manage the second?

We expect, at least I expect and every science fiction movie I have ever seen on the subject has confirmed my expectation, to carry what we know backward with us. Like some Platonic notion of the redevelopment of the soul now that it's stuck in our mortal bodies, only in reverse. I like to believe I have a perfect retrospective knowledge of my life, having a pretty good memory and already having lived up to age forty-three years and eleven months. All I have to do is fix it, revise.

In what way? To revise just the first big event will, of course, erase all the others anyway. I could never find my way back to this very present where most of the time I'm a satisfied guy. No, what I want, what I guess we all want when we crawl back through a hole in time, is to recover time itself. Back behind us are vast open tracts of empty, wasted time. All the things we wish we had done, all the things we now wish we could do thoroughly or well could be managed in a jiffy if we could just get hold of some of those enormous amounts of slack time.

High-school study halls, rides on buses to and from ball games. Three courses in educational psychology. Meandering after-dinner arguments. Card games, board games. Crummy novels. Crummy movies. Television. Three years of long-distance drives to see a woman who didn't love me. Trying to fix cars and appliances and ending up taking them to the shop more broken than they were before. Football practice. Committee meetings. Plane rides. Layovers on plane rides. Avoiding making unpleasant phone calls. Moving. Cleaning up the house for friends' and relatives' visits. Yard work. Waiting for doctors, for barbers, for my wife, for my car to get out of the shop.

Somehow this is not exactly what I meant. Somehow I expected to find my past time buried in such manageable shapes that it would become clear once they were excavated that I could have and should have written a couple of successful novels; mastered Latin, the saxophone, and piano; read the good books and seen the good movies. Led, in short, the kind of productive life I have envied on other people's curriculum vitae.

Yet to wish it this way is to accept missing the small black bear that ambled across the road in front of our truck, the very truck now down the bank, on top of Murphy Dome. Or the moose that was in the road on the way back from an abbreviated fishing trip when my wife fell in the river and we had forgotten our extra clothes. So that trip was futile, a waste of time, two hours of driving for a few minutes of fishing. But we saw a moose and a bear, and in this world, in these times, moose and bear are wonders to see, on the verge of slipping from us so quickly we will scarcely have time to realize our regret for having let them go.

To wish it this way is to accept missing the good laughs and cockeyed hope in a Buddy Nordan short story, reread and reread again at two o'clock in the morning when I can't get to sleep. Missing my expeditions to collect hubcaps from the ditches all around Blacksburg, Virginia, and missing my regret at giving the whole bunch of them away. Accidental moments of illumination that may be more plentiful in my scattered and disorganized life. Just as I regret selling my '64 Chevy Malibu and my BMW motorcycle, and wrecking the 1988 red Chevrolet truck.

Though in the larger scheme of things it is relatively minor, a speck of lint, this last moment is what I would like to revise the most right now. To just run the film loop in reverse, the way we did the old eight-millimeter reels shown on a bedsheet in my parents' living room. The last thrill of the evening, to watch ourselves undo all our actions, to back right off the screen into nowhere. My truck flips back onto its left side, then up onto its wheels, and rolls back up the bank, out into the roadway, swerves wildly backward down the road until it reaches the bottom of the hill. There. Let's leave it at that.

Meditation on My Cousin Lou, Dead at Thirty-Three

On December 17, my cousin Lou was running TV cable into a customer's house when he fell from his ladder onto the driveway below. Nobody was home to see his fall, and when the customers returned, they had no idea how long he had lain there unconscious. Lou had a broken neck, a fractured skull, and a cerebral hemorrhage. Two days later he died without regaining consciousness.

Sometime before Lou's death, I had been observing a graduate student teach a class in remedial English. The grad student insisted I play along, so I took out a piece of paper and, following his example, began listing "things I know." This was designed to be an easy exercise leading to some surefire paper topics. And it was working: all around me students were filling their pages with things like "I know I like dark beer better than light beer," "I know pizza is my favorite food," and "I know blue is my favorite color." I wish I could recall what my frame of mind was when I entered that classroom, but I cannot. All I can do is reproduce some elements from my own very short list: "I know my age, the license number on my car, that I don't know more than I know. . . . I know that most of the things I am interested in cannot be known—these are questions about life and death—I know I am alive, I know I will die—I don't know when or where. I know I am hungry, I do know my wife's birthday and my brother's."

On my wife's birthday, my mom called us long-distance and talked to my wife mostly. I was on the extension upstairs listening to this happy talk when my mother broke it off and said, "Bud, I have some bad news to tell you." "How bad?" I asked her, and I was thinking about my dad and his cancer, now thought to be cured but never far out of mind. This was Mom's way of getting to such things, a running start, a chance for me to get braced. "Real bad," she said. "What?" I said to prompt her. "Louis died today," she said; and it took me a while to put it together. "Louis Soos?" I asked her, I remember, because he was the only person I could match with that name and yet that couldn't possibly be right.

I have spent some time trying to explain to myself how this thing happened. There was a ladder and a driveway and some cable that Lou was pulling from the pole down to the eaves of the house. When I finally went to Pocahontas just after Christmas, I even considered driving over to Bluewell to see the place where it happened, except there would be no way to know the house without leaving myself open to what would seem to most a morbid curiosity. But I continue to think of the top of the ladder and the ground and the distance in between. Not a long fall, I would guess, and using the formulas I learned in my high-school physics, I could figure the time it took. Then what would I know?

It seems to me that the brain is amazingly adept at tracking the body's motion. It can chart the progress of an irregularly moving mass and program what steps are necessary to ensure the least damage on landing. It is tempting to imagine this system as one of those computer-screen graphics, so popular in TV commercials these days, that show the motions of a three-dimensional object as it rotates before us. This would be too simple. Because it must be more than just the visual—the eyes would be almost helpless as images flashed past—it must be our very skin that feels the rush of the air and can tell the brain how we must respond. Yet it is a system so effective that I can recall only twice its having failed me: when I was twelve, I fell from a fifteen-foot-high diving platform, and many years later, at twenty-four or so, I had my legs cut out from under me on a basketball court and flipped about eight feet to the floor. Each time I was aware of my brain struggling to take in the tumbling world and to find my body in relation to the ground. But sometimes the brain just can't quite catch up. I found the ground when I hit it.

On the day of the fall, Lou and his wife, Jeanie, planned to begin moving into their new house, the one they had signed the papers on the evening before. The day of his death, in addition to being my wife's birthday, was also Lou's father-in-law's. Somehow we talk about these things. Jeanie says how hard it will be to celebrate this date from now on. But nobody speaks of ironies; they are just abstractions that keep us a safe distance from understanding. So we are forced back onto the facts. His coworkers say he always wore his safety belt and the weather was beautiful. Nobody can explain it.

Maybe we come honestly by this inability to understand, since nobody much dies unexpectedly anymore. There are stillborn infants and crib deaths, but somehow we have made a place for those who are not fully in the world yet, along with the old whose deaths have been secretly anticipated for some time. And in small towns like ours, even the death of the crazy kid who wraps his Camaro around a tree is expected. Those who have been paying attention have seen it coming for some time. But Lou's death caught us all by surprise.

I missed the funeral service. My mother says it was crowded, so crowded that people stood outside the church to be part of it. My brother says it was in bad taste. My guess is that the preacher didn't really know Lou and did the best he could. He was a Full Gospel preacher, probably not trained in modern psychological techniques for coping with grief as a college-educated preacher might have been. And I guess he saw the senseless death of a man everybody agreed was a good man, a good citizen and father, as a chance to remind everybody that this was their fate, too, and that, by the way, they stood a good chance of going to hell.

A Christian woman has written to Ann Landers to tell her what she knows, that God has sent diseases such as AIDS and herpes as a plague on those who break His commandments. She knows because she has been to church and fears God. Ann disagrees. She has been to church and loves God. I confess that I neither fear nor love God but have plenty of questions about what manner of God we are up against here.

My aunt Rose helped Helen raise Lou. Maybe because he had no father, they doted on him. My mother was sure they were spoiling him. And to have watched them raise him, you would have had to agree it was true. There was no toy or game he didn't have. There was no kind of treat they didn't give him, so that my mother was reluctant to let my brother and me go down to Maple Grove to play with him because she didn't want our teeth to fall out from all the Cokes and cookies and tea loaded with sugar.

My aunts continue to take care of my youngest aunt, Barbara or Barbie or Susie; the family calls her all three. She has been retarded and epileptic from birth. She cannot feed herself and has always been incontinent. When she is happy, she gurgles and coos—the flickering TV and the constant presence of one of my aunts keep her happy most of the time. When she is frightened, she moans and cries. Lots of things can scare her; nobody can guess what they might be. Her greatest pleasure is to pull and twist a screen door spring in her dry hands. I can't imagine how many of these springs she must have twisted until they snapped since I've never seen her without one. Like all epileptics, she gradually grows immune to her medication and has serious seizures. Lately, these involve rushed ambulance trips to the hospital in Bluefield. If my dad's youngest brother is in his late fifties, then Barbie must be in her early to mid-fifties. She is a wonder. The doctors say most people as severely retarded as she is don't live beyond their twentieth birthday.

My aunts don't complain about Barbie; they only marvel. The last time she was so sick, they thought she would die. Helen says Lou explained it. Even when he got married, he stayed close; his house was only fifty yards from Rosie and Helen's. Lou said Jesus wasn't ready for Barbie yet.

* * *

In my ignorance, I love to look at schematic diagrams. They are a world of the parallel and the perpendicular, all angles are right angles. Wires cross each other with a bump, a squiggle in a circle makes a light, zigzags mean resistance, and a switch is indicated by a small open gate. This is a symbolic world, though; what we are really talking about is electrons moving at the speed of light along wires, through compressed silicon, tungsten, whatever. We can make their passing so difficult that these electrons produce heat and light. We can open the gate and stop their movement altogether.

Lou was an electrician by trade, a tinkerer by habit. There is a difference. Tinkerers can never really leave things alone. Somehow Lou had managed to wire his VCR into his TVs so that you could watch a movie on cassette or regular TV at the same time on any television in the house. None of his pals from work who pitched in and moved Jeanie could figure out how he did it; they couldn't get it hooked back up his way, either. They'll always have to admit he stumped them on that one.

Me, too. He stumped us all by doing more than what any good electrician can do, read the schematic. He was able to get into the system and see how it was working and build off it. His wife says he used to tell her, "Use a little logic, Jeanie." Which is an answer to half my problem: it explains how he wired up the TV sets. But would that be the same Lou who told Helen that Jesus wasn't ready for Barbie yet?

I have been wondering about how the brain, a series of circuits—it's comforting to think of it in metaphor—turns itself off. What was he thinking, if that is the word, in those two days he lay dying? As on the occasions of my falls, did his brain put all its energy into keeping the body together? How did it give up? Did it know to give up when machines kept a steady respiration going down below against the truth of the messages from the nerves that all was not well?

Articles in *Reader's Digest* say it can now be confirmed that there is a life after death. The brain doesn't really need to turn itself off, exactly. The soul extricates itself like a spaceman whose ship is in distress. Those who have been to the edge of death and come back say there is a long dark tunnel and at the end a great light, and someone will be waiting for us there. Clearly this is the Sweet By-and-By. Those survivors say they felt a sense of peace, of relief. Some have even expressed disappointment at having been dragged back to the living; their lives would never come up to the promise of what was just beyond that tunnel.

I cannot imagine what it might be. What sort of happiness could such a place offer? What kind of heaven would this be where a man who left a wife and two fine sons behind him could even think of his own happiness? Preachers assure us that the dead understand all. Through that understanding will all then be rendered okay, just fine? Maybe it will be like being really stoned or standing under a hot shower after a hard workout. The brain will be so full of the fluff of understanding that it will forget.

It will be so full that it won't even wonder what sort of God it is that could come up with a system where kids will go through life without a dad and have to make the best of it. It will be so full that it will not have the space available to wonder how those kids will turn out when it, being pure essence or whatever, will not be able to do a blessed thing about it.

I have read the Book of Job many times and remain dissatisfied. God is bigger than you are is what it says. And I have read Ecclesiastes, too. I have no awe, and I am not resigned.

When I was young and discovered I had no faith, I was at first euphoric. It's nice to have no rules; the sensation of freedom can be pleasing. It was equally pleasant for a while to discover I wasn't out in the dark by myself, that other minds had traveled the same road. There was even a temptation to gloat at the expense of believers.

• • •

Lou's older boy, Jason, wants to be with his mother all the time now; he's afraid she will leave him, too. Brandon is so young you wouldn't think he would understand anything at all, but he won't sleep. Only my aunt Helen can soothe him; she is good at it, having been at it so long with Barbie. You could say she has dedicated her life to soothing. "Jesus wanted him to come home," she says to Jason over and over, and turns to the other adults for confirmation: "Ain't it?"

"Yes," I tell her. At such times, I would welcome belief if it came to me like the gentle pressure on the bladder when I have to go to the bathroom. But it doesn't come; it doesn't even want to come.

Maybe, as Pascal said, God has just checked out, is perhaps in another part of the universe and will get back to us. I think of the jugglers on the *Ed Sullivan Show*, the ones whose finale was to get dozens of dinner plates spinning on top of long metal rods. While the architect of this scheme moves from plate to plate, setting them up and getting them started, others begin to wobble, to loop out of control. One of those plates is us. Maybe God will come rushing back and give us another spin just in the nick of time.

Maybe such signs as snowflakes and recombinant DNA are here to show me that God has been around. I should give these beautiful patterns more notice; we couldn't be the universe's biggest happenstance. The woman who wrote Ann Landers could be right, such a God might be angry with the mess we have made of this world. Angry at me and others who don't believe. Well, I guess I'm angry too.

◆　◆　◆

Jeanie's new house still looks kind of naked. It's bigger than the old place, and the furniture won't quite fill it up. Jason's kindergarten teacher and her husband, who teaches music, are there. Jason likes school, and his teacher says the atmosphere brightens when he comes into the room. To watch him play, zipping around the room and up the stairs, sliding down them all the while holding a toy man on a motorcycle before him, is to watch his father. I have played on the floor with his dad as the adults talked, as we are talking about Jason's return to school after the holidays, about how he is handling "it." I know that despite all his frenetic activity, he is listening, as we used to listen while the grownups talked, hoping he will hear something that in a sentence might make it all right again.

I am listening too, and looking. The street outside is quiet. People read the paper. They don't save the clipping for the family as they would for a wedding or a birth. But having seen the obituary they stop a little, and when they pass the house, they drop their voices and their eyes. Men who have no words come up to my father and press money into his hand, for the kids, for their college. The cable company will match every dollar.

I think this combination of grief and generosity is Pocahontas's way of coming to terms with Lou's death. He was a good man, a good husband and father. He helped his neighbors in small ways. Small-town people may understand these acts are the truest indicators of a person's character, and through them, they will remember Lou.

And I will still be wondering why he died. His sudden death momentarily stripped my mind and left the feelings bare. I remember walking out the gate, the cold weight of the latch in my hand, the cracks of the sidewalk through my shoe. The new house is on Moore Street, and the previous owners cut down the big maple in front. They couldn't get the stump out; cut to ground level, it remains.

Glamour and Romance

O Youth, the glamour of it, the romance.

—Joseph Conrad

It was in the gym that I discovered the romance of those epic poems *The Iliad* and *The Odyssey* might be played out in Pocahontas High basketball, their nearest visible manifestation. I was a boy with a hyperactive imagination, and I was all too willing to lift a basketball game up and away from the day-to-day life that surrounded me.

Still, I wondered how it was possible that a boy could put on a basketball uniform, step onto a floor, and be magically transformed, not only in the mind of spectators but in his own mind as well. When Van Gentry stood on the free-throw line in that last home game against Big Creek in 1962, did he feel the weight of our expectations? Did he take up that weight joyfully, knowing he was golden at that moment? When he made those shots, had he launched himself forever to a place above our ordinary lives?

A basketball uniform, especially the uniform worn in the '50s and '60s, was a skimpy thing. The satin shorts, the sleeveless jersey with ample arm openings called attention to, exaggerated even, whatever shape the body inside it took. A lanky bag of bones looked even more so in such a uniform.

Yet the boys I admired did manage to put on their uniforms and achieve the miracle of transcendence before my very eyes. It helped that their uniforms fit better than mine, that, unlike some of the teams they played against, everybody's matched and was in good condition. The boys on the varsity made their uniforms their own. They sweated through their jerseys, pulled their shirttails out and wiped their faces on them, reached down to their ankles and dried their sweaty hands by pulling them up along the long socks until their uniforms became extensions of their very skins.

Mostly, though, those boys managed to transcend themselves in the most literal way. They forgot. They forgot they were skinny and frail. The ball became the center of their universe and chasing it up and down the court, claiming possession of it, following its flight to the goal, became the only thing that mattered to them. At such moments of high concentration, they ran as if there were no wall at the end of the court to stop them, they jumped as if they might fly up and above the rim, even the backboard. They threw passes that sailed the length of the court or bounced slyly between two defenders. They shot arcing jump shots from distances well beyond the free-throw circle, their arms extended long after the ball had flown free—a kind of supplication for a perfect trajectory to the goal.

Or at least that's how I remember it. Through my memory, I have transformed what's left of an actual history into myth. Within that myth are the qualities of glamour and romance. *Glamour*, it turns out, is a Scots word meaning magic, enchantment, the ability to deceive the sight. And romance might be thought of as an exaggeration, an invention—though to me it is a story, a story raised far above the ordinary. In my boyhood, I'm not sure I could have helped myself from reconfiguring the world in this magical, extraordinary way. In my adulthood, I have to wonder how well it served me then, and whether it might serve me now in a world where glamour and romance are in short supply.

◆　◆　◆

Some years ago, the disgruntled football player Duane Thomas called his coach Tom Landry "a plastic man." As it happened, I knew a guy who got a tryout with the Dallas Cowboys right about that time. He didn't make the cut, but he came back to school reporting that Tom Landry was a fine fellow with a good sense of humor. I don't doubt it.

On Sunday afternoons I used to imagine Johnny Unitas drawing his pass patterns in the dirt as the Baltimore Colts staged another last-minute comeback try. If the Colts could only get the ball at the end of the game, anything seemed possible. I wonder if Duane Thomas wasn't subject to some of those same imaginings himself. After the first Super Bowl, the story went around that Green Bay Packer end Max McGee had pitched a drunk the night before the game, only to pull his hungover self together by the next afternoon and play a remarkable game. Just so. Hadn't Knute Rockne dragged George Gipp out of a South Bend poolroom before big games? As Joseph Conrad would say, the glamour of it, the romance of it! Youth overcoming great obstacles even when youth itself set the obstacles in the way.

Conrad puts glamour in his character Marlow's mouth as he tells a tale of his own youth as the second mate of a sailing ship that in mid-journey burned to the waterline and sank. In this instance, Conrad's lived experiences and Marlow's fictional ones were very nearly the same. In giving him his own story to tell, Conrad made Marlow the kind of man who could both relish his youth and gently mock it.

Two versions of Marlow inhabit Conrad's short story "Youth." One is the older man telling the tale. He sees the *Judea* as she truly is, a leaky, broken-down tub that has seen better days. He sees the captain as befuddled and slightly inept, though well-meaning. And he sees the series of near-disasters that befall the ship as, at best, a running bad joke against all aboard.

But the younger Marlow living the tale looks on the *Judea* and sees her glorious motto: Do or Die. He sees the misadventures as trials to be met and mastered. Sailing into Bangkok harbor in a fourteen-foot boat with a sail made from a coat is the culmination of a grand adventure.

The world of Conrad's "Youth" is narrowed to that ship, the *Judea*. Is it any different on a basketball court? As the aperture of experience is narrowed to a world of elemental actions, actions with clear meanings and expectations, qualities may emerge seemingly closer to the truth of who we are. I think I believe this. A closely guarded player makes the clutch shot or he doesn't; a team beats a press without panicking or it doesn't. A team wins a close game or it doesn't.

I think Conrad might agree that the same Marlow regarding his boyish self in "Youth" has somehow, by making a success of his first command even if it is only a long boat, made the first steps to ready himself for the sight years later of Kurtz's collection of human heads impaled on stakes. Once again, Conrad's fiction is not so far from the facts of his own trip up the Congo River. But even *Heart of Darkness* is a distillation. So too is *The Iliad*, where war isn't glorified but magnified through Homer's narrow lens.

In "Youth," the younger Marlow would make his story a romance if he could—a story outside the bounds of ordinary life—if his older self did not keep pulling him back with the all-too-ordinary details of this tale—the ship laid up and in need of caulking, the presence of the grumpy first mate and the captain's motherly wife. And a reader finds himself pushed and pulled between the two. For all his mockery, the older Marlow allows his younger self a transcendent moment as he and his exhausted crew awaken and look up on the dock into the faces of the men of the East, each a mystery to the other.

◆　◆　◆

On the all-sports channels at the end of a day (though with twenty-four-hour coverage, does a day ever end?), a person might see a cobbled-together highlight film of every spectacular play from a whole day's worth of basketball. Dunk after dunk, block after block, buzzer beater after buzzer beater. Who can care when acts once thought to be exceptional become commonplace?

Unlike my brother, the avid reader of *VeloNews*, the subscriber to the expanded cable TV package so he can watch every stage of the Tour de France, I tend to watch cycle racing as warily as any other contemporary sport, watch out of the skeptical corner of my eye. Still, Floyd Landis's ride on the last mountain stage of the 2006 race inspired me and lifted me up. For a moment I was taken in by everything I wish sport might be: his breakaway. A lone eagle soaring above all others, finding strength within himself to make an incredible comeback on that most difficult terrain. Courage and determination. An athlete asking much of himself and finding the strength within to triumph.

As Roland Barthes, that surprising fan of the Tour, put it, sport at its best is "the euphoria of men raised for a while above the constitutive ambiguity of everyday situations." Here was the very kind of moment Barthes and I were hoping for. It couldn't last, could it, dragged down as it was by the sleazy allegations and denials of doping that have become expected in modern sport? Will people ever again line the route as the Italian fans once did for their hero, Fausto Coppi, sweeping the road with their coats to protect some future rider from punctures?

◆　◆　◆

Whether Pocahontas lost to Haysi or beat Big Creek, we all, parents and kids alike, stumbled from the gym at game's end wrung out from catharsis.

In the bleachers, I had sat transfixed by the glamour, the romance of the game before me. That these players were on a stage, that they were the center of a drama that consumed not only them but the people of our town who crowded into the bleachers, seemed lost on them. Their only moments of self-awareness were those when they were whistled for a foul. In those days a player was required to acknowledge he had committed a foul. So with a look of stricken amazement, a player would often hold one hand to his chest, to his number, and raise his other—a victim of an unfair call by the referee appealing to the larger audience for a better verdict.

Aren't glamour and romance qualities of life suspended in the ever-present, of an expectation that the now will always be now? These games from my boyhood remain as present for me as they were on the day they were played. Their outcomes cannot change; their heroic feats and tragic blunders remain. I wonder, then, how it feels to be Jerry West or Bill Russell, how it feels to have so many recorded images of yourself in the not-now. What's it like to watch yourself on film doing things you know you could never do again? Can the glamour that my heroes seemed to possess, that held me as a boy, for a high school basketball season of twenty games or so, persist? Should it?

Imagine a boy, maybe every boy who ever hoped for a moment of transcendence on a basketball floor. Maybe he is Pocahontas guard Eddie Goss shooting jump shots at the lonely goal set up in the bottomland below his parents' house: "Time is running out . . . five . . . four . . . three . . . Goss with the ball at the head of the key . . . he shoots . . . will it drop? No! It's short. But wait! Goss gets his own rebound . . . the short jumper is up! It's good! The crowd goes wild." With every practiced shot, he anticipates the grander moment in the making.

In meeting the players of the great Pocahontas teams I have been struck by their tranquillity in repose. Among the stars from those teams, almost all have made a satisfactory life on their own terms. How much of this is a result of playing a simple game? How much of it is a result of being part of a team whose players made the steals, made the shots when the game was on the line?

Unlike the great team of 1962–63, which could rout opponents if it was in the right mood or lose to a weaker team if it wasn't, the more successful team of 1965 won efficiently, consistently, night after night. In my senior season we mostly lost, were rarely blown out, most often losing by a few points. You might say we found a way to lose consistently, to fold up reliably at some crucial moment in the game.

◆ ◆ ◆

Just how much do moments of transcendence depend on having an audience? When Sam Caldwell made his three-quarter-court shot to beat Honaker in the final second, he was golden among his teammates and classmates. The next day, Coach Tommy Lucas taped a bill on the floor on the spot Sam had shot from. If he could replicate his shot, Sam could have the money. Was it a five? A twenty? Over the years, the denomination had to grow in my memory to hedge glamour against inflation. Regardless, Sam couldn't come close in the three tries allotted him. His feat of the night before became all the more remarkable in our eyes. When it counted—when the team, the school, the town was counting on him—Sam made his shot go in.

My coach friend Ernie Pope used to call remarkable play, when a player's shots find the goal, his passes find the open man, when the player's every action is a right action, "going unconscious." The crowd and his teammates sense his heightened powers and turn to him. And his opponents sense it, too, but can't seem to do much about it.

Going unconscious, playing within yourself, is an aesthetic as much as an athletic gesture. The Champion's Light, mythmakers call it, something that has been recognized since ancient times. It's what Homer says of Achilles when he returns to battle so the Achaeans might salvage the body of Patroclus. Athena, interceding, "bound his head with golden cloud, and made / his very body blaze with fiery light" (*The Iliad*, book 18, lines 207–208). Seeing him illuminated so, the Trojan warriors quit the field of battle.

．　◆　．

In the dressing room afterward, the uniform that meant so much minutes before is dropped on the floor for the manager to pick up. A player who has played hard will hit the shower and wash the game away. One who has not played at all will slip on his street clothes and silently go.

Out in the gym, the bleachers have been pushed back; the janitors are running their wide dust mops, pushing the stray popcorn boxes and empty soda cups along. This is aftermath. The air is still overheated, but the crowd has gone. Some parents, a girlfriend or two are waiting. But when a player returns to the gym now, he must return as his most ordinary self, regardless of how he has performed that night.

Transcendence is a fleeting, fragile thing.

Such transcendent moments never happened for me. In high school I was such a bag of bones that I wonder now what it would have taken to overcome the mere physical fact of my boyhood body and become a hero on a basketball court. I would first of all have had to overcome myself. My first basketball uniform was a baggy orange jersey adorned with the number nine and nothing else, no team name, nothing. And the nine was huge, big enough to go on a football jersey. The armholes came nearly to where the shirt tucked into my black shorts, shorts of a uniform rather than plain old gym shorts by virtue of a piece of orange trim. The leg openings were ample so a boy sitting on the bench might be offering a view of his jockstrap and who knew what-all else. We had no warm-up outfits, and to step from the locker room into the gym was like taking the walk from the dressing room at Falls Mills Dam before jumping into that cold lake. I spent almost all of my ninth-grade year sitting on a bench in our empty gym or an equally empty gym at another school, conscious of every bone in my body uselessly on display.

Often I experienced the very opposite of transcendence. In a JV game against Whitewood, the score tied with seconds remaining, I had played fairly well so far. Approaching the man I was guarding on their inbounds play, I stamped my feet, a little war dance to let him know I was ready for whatever might come. When he only laughed, it set me back; wasn't I a silly goose? Next thing I knew he had slipped around me for the ball and an easy basket.

Playing well, then, turned out to be harder than it looked. The romance of spectating is found in that distance between the stands and the floor. The glamour of playing, brought out by accomplishment, is rarely available for losers.

* * *

Over my workbench is a poster, a scene from the 1924 Tour de France. Ottavio Bottecchia and a second are pictured in a tight switchback climbing the Col du Galibier. The road is hard-packed dirt. A snowfield is in the foreground and in the back, cold mountains against a hard sky. There has been no parade of sponsors' cars filled with pretty girls tossing souvenirs to the crowd. There is no crowd. There are no following team cars carrying coaches, mechanics, and spare parts. The riders carry spare tires looped in a figure eight through their arms and across their backs. A few spectators line the route bundled in overcoats. A few bicycles lie beside the road. These spectators have come more to witness than to cheer.

I wonder, even if he didn't know it, whether this picture is close to what Duane Thomas—what all of us true believers in the romance and glamour of sport—had in mind? Nothing in this picture speaks to scientific training practices featuring computer-generated workout schedules, strategic and tactical decisions dictated by a coaching staff. Here are athletes true only to themselves, present only in their moment.

* * *

Yet oftentimes audience matters. It's not that transcendence requires an audience, but that the events surrounding it matter. The remarkable feats a player might perform in practice, in a pickup game on a Sunday morning cannot count in the same way when there are no witnesses. So I believe. Playing well in practice doesn't count. And good play counts in a game because the honor of the team, the school, the town is at stake. To win is to be recognized, recognized as somebody doing something.

I have had my own minor Galibier moments. Once on a spring break cycle tour, I climbed to the summit of Ola Mountain in the Ouachitas of Arkansas on an unseasonably hot day; another time I climbed the Brushy Mountains near my Appalachian home—two steep climbs on loaded bikes along roads twisted with switchbacks. At the top, unnoticed and alone, I rested long enough to take a swig from my water bottle and began my descent. If there is romance to be sought at all in such episodes, it may be found only through the telling.

It's the great gift of literature that it can make transcendence happen. Achilles has achieved his lasting fame thanks only to Homer, who preserved his actions in a more permanent form. As for Marlow, his story is more accurately a chronicle of failure. Conrad has allowed him to recast the story of a ship lost at sea, a cargo gone undelivered into an adventure. Achilles and Marlow have had their transcendent moments through language transferred to us readers, their witnesses. Bottecchia lives on by the grace of a grainy black-and-white photograph.

I have saved a clipping from the Tazewell County *Free Press* my mother sent me in the year before her death. Mark Little, a player from Pocahontas, had bested the school's career scoring record, a record held just then, in fact, by a girl, Carrie Dawson. I saw from his picture that he was a wiry boy, smallish, very like other Pocahontas ball players I have known. Later on a visit home, my mom had pointed him out to me, just a kid stuck in a hall waiting, waiting for something or somebody. I looked for the Champion's

Light around him but could not see it. I guess I would have had to be there in that overheated gym.

• • •

At what age can a person look back on the passion of his youth with good humor and irony? And under what circumstances?

I think of Big-Eye Jennings in his Milwaukee apartment carefully unfolding for me his clipping from the 1961 Tazewell County Tournament. I wonder if it is an emblem of a boyhood left incomplete when he ran off to join the navy—a boyhood he can't get back, a boyhood that had its moments of glamour and romance, but such moments were never enough.

My mother believed the purpose of sport was to teach character. If it is so, a person may learn it best when he loses, when he fails. I wonder if my own failures on the basketball court have something to do with my mulish persistence in playing at sport as long as I'm able to stand. Still, I often go out expecting to fail. It's a psychology made from an odd combination of determination and self-doubt and has served me best in lonely sports—long-distance running, cycling, cross-country skiing, sculling. And it has served me best when I am truly alone, when there's nobody to answer to but me, when because of my age and limited skills, the only available triumph is in finishing.

If there is a revelation in "Youth," it's found when the elder Marlow suddenly lets go of his ironic tone: "Ah! The good old time—the good old time. Youth and the sea. Glamour and the sea! The good, strong sea, the salt bitter sea, that could whisper to you and roar at you and knock the breath out of you."

Yes, when the strong sea knocks you down, there is no time for irony. Glamour is felt more than known, romance recognized only after the fact. Such trials are good things, though, to have lived, to have experienced.

It's unlikely that on our deaths, athletic contests will be held in our honor, or great funeral pyres, fed by sacrificed animals and enemies, will cremate our corpses. Most likely we will die quietly in our beds, whatever transcendent moments we experienced forgotten by all save ourselves.

In truth, I'm not sure transcendence is available in the visible world. We make it happen in our heads and hearts, we feel it, we come to know it and cherish it. It is ours to remember and never allow to die.

Other People's Pain
and My Own

I must start with the cat. The cat who (yes, who) last week tangled with a fox out by the woodpile. By the time I arrived on the scene, damage had been done. I gathered the hissing and snarling cat, fully puffed up for maximum effect, in my arms; shooed off the fox, which was reluctant to give ground; and brought the cat in. Back on her feet, she hobbled to a safe corner with her left hind leg turned under her. Oh, oh, oh, Margot cried, while the cat said nothing at all.

Somewhere between Margot's empathetic cries and the cat's silence sits the question: How to know the pain felt by another? And what, if anything, can be done about it?

In 1940, James D. Hardy, Harold C. Wolff, and Helen Goodell, scientists at Cornell University, invented the dolorimeter, a device to indicate, if not pain itself, our measured responses to it. A person might be subjected to heat, pressure, electric shock, or blows from a blunt instrument while the dolorimeter recorded the intensity of each response. Though scientists had moved beyond the dolorimeter by the early 1950s, any interested person can purchase one from Amazon, but might find a cheaper buy on eBay.

My brother, when he was around six or so, cut himself pretty severely in the ankle on a piece of broken bottle. It was a Sunday afternoon. My mom, dad, and I were still at the dinner table—lunch was our big meal on Sundays, right after church. We could hear my brother's wailing from all the way out back behind the house.

His crying went on and on. Little boys crying wolf was a favorite family motif. Finally, my mom said, "Go see what's bothering him." There he was—sitting on a stone wall all the way at the bottom of our hill, maybe a hundred yards away—bawling. And with blood running down his ankle into his shoe.

In the house I grew up in, pain was something best ignored. "Go ahead and cry," our mother told us; "see if that changes anything." Maybe she was right, maybe it didn't.

If stoicism was advocated, it was also demonstrated. My father's father was the model for all of us. He had died two weeks before I was born, and I know little of him, royal hussar in the Austro-Hungarian army, coal miner, patriarch of a family of eight. I do know this: Out in the yard, cutting kindling, he chopped off the tip of his finger with an ax. He picked up the tip and threw it to the chickens before he went to the doctor. Another time, a piece of kindling flew up and hit him between the eyes, opening a big gash. My grandmother found him in front of a mirror with thread and a needle from her sewing basket, trying to stitch himself up.

Pain might be *sharp, cutting, lacerating*. And with the right tools wrongly applied, perhaps all of these at once.

Once while skiing on the university trails, I had a collision on a blind corner. We ran into each other at a pretty good clip, and both fell backward from the contact. As he fell, the other guy's ski pole swung up and clipped me right above the ear. I saw stars, and the blow opened up a half-inch cut, which like all scalp wounds began bleeding like crazy. I said, "That hurt." Ashamed the moment the words came out of my mouth, I got up and skied on. My grandfather's fingertip, by the way, could have been reattached, but that, too, seems to be part of the lesson: once pain is visited on you, get over it and move on.

Because pain was not an acceptable condition in our house, because it was not an acceptable topic of conversation, I have no way to explain it to myself or understand it. What is pain and what is discomfort? What is in our bodies and what is in our heads?

The trivial annoyance of sitting in an airplane seat for the long transcontinental flight is grind enough if a person is six-six, but what's the value of complaining? It won't make the legroom any better, won't make the seat back stop hitting me in the middle of my neck, won't ease my bony rear.

The McGill Pain Questionnaire is one of the instruments, an instrument made of words, designed to supersede the dial on the dolorimeter. It offers a battery of choices for a person's responses, each designed to name a variety of pain. As far as descriptions of the pain itself, the McGill Questionnaire offers *mild, discomfort, distressing, horrible,* and *excruciating.* Never mind that of these words only *excruciating* has an immediate association with pain in my mind. I wonder if the frustratingly cramped airline seat is really only mild rather than uncomfortable, as I suggested earlier. And I am surprised that in somebody's view, discomfort is a form of pain.

My dad home from the hospital after his first operation for lung cancer had to struggle up the stairs to my parents' bedroom, leaning on my shoulder. He was tired; he was weak; the surgery had not gone as expected. When he got to the top of the stairs, he collapsed on the floor, and I did not know how to pick him up or help him up without hurting him more. It turns out there is a way to help a person back to his feet with the help of a straight-backed chair. I know that now. When we made it to the edge of the bed, he dropped more than sat down. He was breathing hard, wheezing, clearly in pain from his incision and maybe from the incisions inside that took part of one lung. Can a person feel pain in the lungs themselves? I don't know. "I'll bet you never thought you'd ever see your old dad like this," he said. I struggled for something to say because he was right.

Pain is *tender.*

We might ask the cat, Does your leg hurt, or is it just unable to move the way it used to? Are you in pain when you lie in your cat lounge or on the furniture, or is your rest easeful? If she could answer, would it change anything?

At the senior center my mom directed, she led an exercise program for the few willing. Sitting in chairs, the seniors threw their arms out in front of them and over their heads, kicked out their legs. "I know it hurts," she hollered at them; "at our age something always hurts."

The night before my dad's second lung surgery, I called him on the phone. "Are you sure you want to do this?" I asked him. "The man says it's got to be done. It's got to be done." My dad was a man of his time and place, and doctors' orders were received with a mixture of resignation and relief, as if a person might pass the burden of suffering into the hands of that wise man.

Pain can be *spreading*.

While Dad had originally had part of the diseased lung removed, this time a different doctor took the whole thing—how it should have been done the first time, the surgeon confidently told my brother. And for a while it looked like he was right, but my dad developed aspiration pneumonia. For months he slipped between a bed on the general medical floor and one in intensive care where he breathed with the help of a ventilator—the vent.

Kierkegaard might agree there is a distinction between depression and despair. Depression, even a morose Scandinavian might admit, is an illness that can be treated. As a doctor friend told me, "We have drugs for that." Despair, though, is a natural human condition because we of all the animals live with the knowledge of our mortality. Would this be a kind of chronic pain? Healthy people mistrust the idea. People with chronic pain are shirkers, slackers, wimps. Maybe Kierkegaardian despair falls into the same category. Nothing wrong with you that a good kick in the ass won't cure. I have that thought every time I watch an Ingmar Bergman movie.

Exposure to that kind of pain can be *exhausting* in itself. *Suffocating.*

When my mom fell and broke her leg, she scooted herself down the stairs on her rear and sat by the front door banging on the wall until her neighbor heard her. She seemed more chagrined at the way she did it (she fell backward off her bed, where she was standing to change a light bulb), than in pain. But the break did hurt, and getting around on the leg hurt. The broken leg led to a knee replacement, and that hurt, too. A *throbbing* kind of pain. Despite her imprecations against whining, she did her share. But she got up and walked, first with a walker, and then with a cane, and then on her own. *Nagging* pain. And *miserable*, too.

Once I was driving along with a friend on the way to a day hike when the cell phone rang. It was my stepdaughter calling to tell me she had suffered a second miscarriage. Would I tell her mom? She felt she couldn't. I tried to calm her as best I could from four thousand miles away at sixty miles per hour, and then I called Margot. I tried to calm her, too, so that when she talked to her daughter she might help alleviate the pain rather than allow it to spiral down deeper. Now my stepdaughter is raising a lovely child. But has the pain from those miscarriages, the grief for children she will never get to see grow up, passed?

In the McGill Pain Questionnaire, temporal pain might be *flickering, quivering, pulsing, throbbing, beating,* or *pounding,* each word associated with an ascending number. What Kierkegaard believed was that despair described a necessary form of pain. Through our recognition of our inherent despair, we would seek strategies to confront it, to keep it under control; we would seek to lead meaningful lives. *Heavy* pain. However, the questionnaire offers no menu of words for measuring the effects of enduring pain.

Some years after my dad's death, I read an article suggesting that long-term use of a vent might cause patients to have horrendous nightmares or hallucinations. Once off the vent, many patients experience posttraumatic stress. Through all that long, dark journey, days beyond lost days, what had gone on up there in Dad's head? And would that, too, be a kind of pain, the confusion of being seemingly lost forever in a trackless woods? Pain *terrifying* and *frightful.*

Even under heavy sedation, my dad tried to self-extubate from the vent every chance he could. One day we came into his room and found him in arm restraints. The vent—our family came to dread the word. We all made living wills. *Gnawing* pain.

When I crashed on my bicycle and broke my femur, shattered the trochanter—the bone at the top, the ball that goes into the socket to make the hip joint—I picked myself up and tried to get back on my bike. I had places to go and things to do and was already late. The next morning, Margot and I were to drive to Maine and get married there. But I couldn't get my leg over the top tube of the bike, so I sat on a nearby bench and called Margot, asking her to come fetch me.

Using my bike as a cane, I walked to an intersection where she could pick me up. Once in the car, I told her I thought if we stopped at a drug store where I could buy some ibuprofen and a cane, I would be fine. She drove me to the emergency room instead, where it turned out I needed a wheelchair to get myself inside. In the crowded ER, I managed to hobble to the intake desk where I was asked to rate my pain on a scale of one to ten. Feeling lucky, I said seven. Truly, this was merely *troublesome* pain.

When I watch her hobbling along, I ask myself if the cat feels pain when she is walking, if she feels pain when she is at ease? If her injuries cause constant pain or discomfort or if the nerves that control her tail and some of the muscles in her leg have simply been turned off?

Pain may be *bright* or *dull*.

When our mom's respiration dropped below a certain level, a horn, a horn sounding very like the horn on a clown car, started honking at the nurses' station around the corner. They ignored it, knowing the vent—the vent, something she had explicitly told us she did not want—would take up the slack. They were right; the vent could keep pushing oxygen in, pulling carbon dioxide out for months, years. Despite the sedating meds, my mom's frustration came through. She would make a fist and pound it against the side of her bed. Her arms, too, were trapped in restraints. *Tugging* pain.

The cat seems to have lost much of her mischievous spirit. She no longer slips onto the kitchen table to lick the butter when we aren't looking. She has discontinued her nightly inspection of the kitchen counters as soon as we go to bed, her raid known to us not by the silent leap up to the three-foot countertops, but by the resounding thump when she lands back on the floor. She no longer stands on her hind legs at the foot of the bed to bop us with her paws, her act an insistence that breakfast be served. She spends more time sleeping, less time poking around where she doesn't necessarily belong.

After my brother's open-heart surgery, he slipped into atrial fibrillation a time or two. The heart, which I'm told has no feeling, sent its irregular rhythm through his arteries. Did this hurt, or did it just feel wrong? When he coughed in response to the excess pollen in the air, he grabbed a pillow and pushed it to his chest. Rather than sit by and watch him, I ran out to buy him tea and honey. I doubt if his pain was lessened when out of my sight. And I wonder if it is possible for pain to be caught like disease from others. *Radiating* pain?

We learned about my stepdaughter's first miscarriage by phone, on the road, at a gas station filling the tank. The connection was bad; we drove out of town until we came to an overlook, an arresting view under other circumstances. Margot did her best to ease her daughter's pain, and I did my best to ease Margot's. We drove on. Back on that stretch of road some years later, we found ourselves searching for the overlook. Surely the site should have been etched into our memories. But we couldn't say for certain where it was we'd pulled off and made the call. Could it be that sometimes pain is *fleeting*?

At last, pain did defeat my mom. The carcinoid tumor in her intestine went undetected while it pumped out enzymes at irregular intervals that would double her over. Somewhere in the third round of tests to find the tumor, the tumor found itself by making a hole in her small intestine. She had submitted to yet another test the day before, had eaten a pleasant lunch afterward with the friend who'd driven her. The following morning, she told me over the phone that while her pain at that moment was pretty bad, roughly translated from our family lexicon as *excruciating*, she planned to take some pain medicine (she would have seen the medicine itself as an indication of surrender) and go to work. She wound up in the emergency room instead. Pain both *searing* and *dreadful*.

The cat stubbornly works at making her left leg behave. She walks several steps, gingerly putting weight on the damaged leg, and then collapses into a sit. I am hesitant to call this effort an intentional strategy on her part or even something more primitive such as willpower, things we humans might ascribe to our own efforts at rehabilitation. The cat probably just wants her leg to work the way it did before.

When people ask me if it hurt to break my hip, I say some smart-ass thing. I say, it didn't exactly feel good. Or I wouldn't stand in line to do it again.

My dad lived a little over a year after he finally got out of the hospital. His one remaining lung struggled to keep him going. When I had a cold, my head stuffed with snot, unable to sleep, I thought, *This is what he must feel like on a good day.* Along the line, his pain passed beyond *tiring* to *exhausting*.

The cat walks with a limp. But her normal gait returns to her in fits and starts. She will even run a few steps when the pantry door opens. So far, though, she has not assayed any of the galloping sprints through the house she was wont to undertake for no good reason we could discern.

When I pulled a muscle in my back, I wasn't skiing or riding my bike, or rowing, or doing any of the things doctors sometimes tell guys my age they shouldn't do, or shouldn't do so much or so intensely. Instead, I did it pulling a duffle bag from behind the seat of my truck. I admit I was on my way to ski, and went ahead and skied anyway, thinking as I always do that I could stretch the muscle as I went, that I would push on through and the pain would go away.

Of the options from the McGill Questionnaire, I would describe my pain as *flickering, jumping,* and *flashing. Piercing.* It might be *fearful* or *frightful.* Cruel? A person might say so. Certainly annoying and troublesome, and at times—unexpected, unpredictable times—*intense.*

Though none of those words explains why I threw my reading glasses against the wall. I was simply trying to make myself comfortable enough to read in bed. But I was thinking that this back damage, as yet undiagnosed, could signal the end of much of what I love most in life—the long solitary skis and bike rides, and just as important, the long, complicated skeins of thought that result from these moving meditations. I rarely intend to go off in search of ideas, but somehow I find them out there. What if I couldn't? Couldn't go, couldn't be who I had always been?

I told myself as I lay waiting for my MRI that I could block the pain from my broken hip for long periods of time if I could just stay focused. This much is true up to a point. A nurse came in and looked at my chart, looked at how I rated my pain, and said, "That's not right, I saw you when you were admitted, you're a ten." Eventually, fatigue comes into play, and no matter how tough, how fit a person may think he is, pain breaks through.

Pain is suffering. Suffering is life. Did we really need the Buddha to tell us that? My dad's last bout with pneumonia killed him while he lay in the hospital declining to be put on the vent again. He was tired of suffering even if he was not tired of life. What else was he to do?

If my pain with the broken hip was, as the nurse suggested, a ten, I sometimes think, *That wasn't so bad.* What else is there? More of the same until it must come to an end. For my dad, stoic, almost cheerful. For my mom, her anger fighting to get past the fog of her medications. For my brother, who successfully got through the pain of his operation. Because there will always be something more. For Margot, for my stepdaughter, for her husband, and even for their toddler. For me.

Margot's cry in response to the cat's pain went straight from somewhere in her limbic brain to her vocal cords and out her mouth. It didn't stop in her higher brain to shop for the right word, nor did it when she cried out in response to news of her daughter's miscarriages, or to the death of our friend Missy. When we need them most, words fail us. The howls, yowls, whimpers, whines, and moans we share with our fellow animals might be the truest responses to pain we can make. And I have to wonder if all our effort at putting language to pain is a foolish endeavor at best. From the toe carelessly stubbed in the dark to the wet blanket of despair draped over us, pain is real, knowable, yet unnamable in any sort of reliably transferable way. It's ours and ours alone to feel and deal with as best we can.

I wonder if what Kierkegaard might say back to me, say to us all, might be, If you're so smart, so human, try to do something about it. Because those electrochemical impulses that are so good at relaying the source and intensity of pain to our brains are very like the ones in our cerebral cortexes that try so hard to explain it. And yet. And yet, I come to this hard place again, and there is no getting past it.

The Man on the Bridge

The man on the bridge could have been my uncle, but he was not.

On the bridge, the bridge that spanned the little coal-black creek that ran through our town, stood a certain kind of man or grown boy. Just down the street was the Cricket and, through the swinging doors in the back, the pool room. On fine spring or summer evenings, a man might have a beer or two, shoot some pool, and then come out and stand among other men and watch the world pass by on the bridge, relish a cigarette or a chew of tobacco, throw the spent butt or spit some juice into the creek.

The man on the bridge could have been among my family, around our Thanksgiving table, receiving the kinds of Christmas gifts my other uncles got, socks, cartons of cigarettes with their festive holiday sleeves featuring arrangements of ornaments and sprigs of evergreen.

My uncle Joe sometimes could be found standing on the bridge. My dad could not.

I passed the men on the bridge on an errand to the bank. Fearsome and gruff, they were best passed looking down.

• • •

My dad and all his brothers and sisters were born at home, in Maple Grove, one house down from the one my aunt Helen lived in most of her life. People called Maple Grove Hunk Town. Hunk Town consisted of one block and a couple of alleys, all lined with company houses—white board-and-batten houses with aquamarine trim. A coal house stood in every yard, a duplex coal house in every duplex yard.

Uncle Joe had been shot up on the beach at Anzio. He may never have been the same after that. That happened before I was born, so I couldn't say.

My parents married in the Hungarian Reformed church that sat on a corner in Maple Grove, with Hungarian and Methodist ministers presiding. After they married, my parents came to live in Butts Hollow, though my mother preferred to call it Spruce Hill. Butts Hollow was a single row of houses all built by George Butt for his children. Except for our house. Our house was a brick duplex built by two of the Ellett brothers for themselves and their wives.

As a boy, my father had gone to work for the Elletts in their general merchandise store. He stocked shelves, ran errands, delivered orders in a horse-drawn wagon and later in a truck. He learned to drive on an Ellett family truck. My mother worked at Elletts', too. After the war, they courted and married. The coal mine closed; the Elletts closed their store. The Ellett brothers scattered. My parents bought into a small store of their own.

Three years after my parents married, I was born; three years after that my brother was born, and a week after that our cousin Louis was born. Unlike my brother and me, he was born at the hospital in Welch, West Virginia, not the closer one in Bluefield.

Louis died in a work-related accident twenty-five years ago, leaving behind a wife and two small sons. His mother, my aunt Helen, was never the same afterward. In some lesser way, neither was my dad.

When Lou was born, my dad's father had been dead for almost three years. His mother, our grandmother, would not live long after Lou's birth. I barely remember her, old in a bib apron trimmed with rickrack, tottering along the wooden walkways that ran around her house where she and my aunts and Uncle Joe kept chickens and ducks. They cooked on a coal stove.

The man on the bridge was said to be the father of my cousin Louis, but I never knew him. Not even his name.

The older I got, the more I saw those men on the bridge were sagging and careworn.

• • •

Helen was sixth of eight siblings. There were five girls and three boys, there were three with blond hair and blue eyes and five with brown hair and brown eyes. Barbie was the youngest, brown hair and eyes, and named for her mother. She wasn't right. She couldn't talk, or feed herself, or control her bowels or bladder. She could be happy for hours twisting an old screen-door spring. We believed she was the way she was as a result of my grandmother's falling down the steep stairs in their company house late in her pregnancy. But my grandmother was getting along in years by then. In truth, we would never know. The fall on the stairs was a good enough explanation. Leave it at that.

I can't remember a time when Barbie was not Helen's responsibility. Rosie worked for my dad at our grocery store. Uncle Joe worked construction when he could find work.

Helen had never been normal, whatever that was in our family, ever since I could remember. When my uncle Joe died, I was a junior in high school. After the funeral, as the day dimmed, there was only family in my aunts' living room, Uncle Yank and Nancy and their adopted little boy; aunts Rosie and Helen; and Barbie, who was my aunt, too, though I never thought of her that way. Barbie's hospital bed took up much of the living room; her presence took up much of Rosie's and Helen's lives.

"Don't go," Helen told us as we got up to leave. "I'm scared." "Of what?" my mother asked her, genuinely concerned. "Joe's ghost." My mother didn't say a word until we were in the car. "Joe's ghost!"

In high-school math class, I learned to think of our family as overlapping sets: my dad and Louis were in the middle, the set of two who held Maple Grove and Butts Hollow together.

As a boy, my dad had been taken into the Ellett household. He stoked their furnace, drove the men to dances when they were young bachelors. My dad wrote clearly with Palmer Method penmanship; he used good grammar. My aunts spoke with lilting Old Country accents. They made cabbage rolls and homemade noodle soup.

At our house, we ate hamburgers. We ate a roast after church on Sundays. Our through-the-wall neighbors were Mr. Frank and Brownie, Elletts grown old.

Though only a week apart, my brother and my cousin were in different grades in school. My mom pushed, pushing us ahead in our lessons, demanding that we do our chores, that we pitch in at the store. She sent us to school early. She had rules that applied to our schoolwork and our after-school games. Once we were on a team, we were on, win or lose, play or sit the bench, for the duration of the season. Unless our grades were bad—then we were off the day we got report cards.

Helen didn't push so much. Going to Maple Grove, to her and Rosie's and Joe's house, to Louis's house, meant cookies and hot cups of tea with lots of sugar, meant more toys than we could dream of for ourselves, meant running a little wild.

Lou was a wiry little kid—he didn't eat right, our mother said— quick mentally and physically. He could have been a good ball player with a little encouragement; he could have been a good musician. He grew up to be a sturdy man and a good citizen. His blond hair turned light brown. I cannot recall the color of his eyes. They must have been brown.

Helen learned to drive on my uncle Albert's old green '49 Ford. It was one of the few things he left the family when he fell down and died of a heart attack in the Pocahontas Fuel Company warehouse. She was a hazard behind the wheel, but Helen drove everywhere, eventually all the way to Myrtle Beach, South Carolina. Barbie rode in the backseat with a rubber sheet under her to protect the upholstery and piles of quilts and blankets to keep her warm. Helen carried her back and forth to the car. That my aunts managed to make their way across the wide world was another mystery to me.

When Helen gave birth to Lou, she wasn't living at home. She was living with Uncle Yank and his wife, Nancy. Whose choice was that?

It wasn't too much sugar in the tea or too many cookies, the too-extravagant Christmas and birthday presents that made my mother want to keep us away from Maple Grove. We knew that, we felt it, but we could not name it.

My other aunts wore dresses, wore stockings rolled up to just below their knees. Helen wore pedal pushers, wore loafers and sandals.

When they were all older, my dad would go down to Maple Grove and sit on the porch with his sisters Rosie and Helen. Time passed and nobody said a word. Sometimes Helen would blurt out a tidbit of gossip. She loved gossip and was always in the know about goings-on around town. Maybe she had paid for the right, having been the occasion of enough gossip herself.

Though I was too innocent to know it then, the men on the bridge were given to gossip.

. . .

"See that man standing on the bridge? That's Louis's father." My high-school girlfriend told me that as we drove by. Where? Which one? How do you know? I was more shocked that such knowledge was in the world and to be had than by the information itself. So surprised, so overcome by my need to know that I cannot recall, was he tall or short, skinny or fat, dark or pale? A likable-looking sort of man? Not likely. As my mother would have it, likable sorts of men were not to be found loafing on the bridge or in the Cricket or its pool room.

Did my uncles Joe and Yank and my dad think they should find this man out and make him do the right thing, assuming they thought the way most people did then, that there was a "right thing" to do? Did anybody expect them to?

It takes two, I know. Maybe the family thought that way, too. Helen: almost thirty when Lou was born. Old enough to know better. Another thing to think.

Whenever I passed over the bridge and a man was standing there, I had to wonder, *Was he the one?*

Lou did not know his father; he did not know his name. Would anything have been different if he had?

Bastard: a word boys flung at each other. Like all those words, I felt its force before I knew what it meant.

Somehow we knew not to ask—not his name, not how it came to be that he was our cousin's father. Somehow our mother threw up a force field stronger than any science-fiction movie could produce. It was there before we ever realized, so strong we never knew to bump against it.

Lou stayed around while my brother and I hightailed it out of the mountains, he to North Carolina, I to Alaska. Lou's boys supplied surrogate grandkids for my dad when my brother and I didn't bring them forth.

Lou named his boys Jason and Brandon. "Jason. Brandon. Whoever heard of Hunky boys named Jason and Brandon?" my mother wondered. And Louis? I knew other Hunky boys and men named Louis, but nobody in our family.

When Lou died, it was a big deal. People liked him. In a town grown old, he was one of the few young people left, one of the few whom an older person could count on for a little help. His boys were precocious, his wife lovely. They had just signed the papers for the mortgage on his house the evening before he died. That sort of irony too easily makes itself tragedy.

What with the obituary in the paper, the funeral service, the public outpouring of grief, the man who was Lou's father must have seen it, must have known. He might have been somewhere in his sixties by then. If he was still around. If he was still alive.

Uncle Joe died in the VA hospital in Salem, Virginia. My aunts Bea and Liz, moved up north, died up there. Barbie died too, and the doctors said it was a wonder she had lived as long as she did. Rosie died. My dad died in the hospital in Bluefield, West Virginia—a newer, better hospital than the one my brother and I had been born in—though he wanted to die at home. Uncle Yank still lives.

Today nobody can be found standing on the bridge.

•　•　•

Helen drifted further. Her house, a swaybacked old company house sinking into the ground, was in part given over to storage of Lou's boyhood toys. Barbie's hospital bed had been taken from the living room, leaving the feeling of hollering across a gulf when I visited there.

In the last year of his life, when my dad was sick and very nearly bedridden, Helen sat with him a good part of every day while my mom went to work. Mostly in silence, I suppose. But she liked daytime TV, the game shows, the talk shows, the soaps, none of which my dad had any patience for. Would she have shaped her needs to fit his wishes? Hadn't she always done that?

Was it her meds or the absence of her meds that caused her not to answer the phone, even if it was a nephew or niece or daughter-in-law? Skittish as a cat except when she went to the post office to pick up what mail she did get and catch up on the gossip, she would have been housebound if people had let her.

Last month Helen died, boxed into a corner by a fistula that would kill her by infection and the operation she proved too frail to survive. She wanted no service, no preacher. She left quietly and took her history with her.

Every family, every little town has its not-so-secret secrets. In every life there are things that have become just what they are. Some things we can know. Some things we don't get to know. Some things don't get found out. That's all I can say.

Naked to the World

When a man dies, an unknown world passes away.
—Antoine de Saint-Exupéry, *Wind, Sand and Stars*

By the time he was my age, Beowulf was dead beneath his barrow. Probably the mice had picked over what was left of his bones. Probably some thief, some less-than-loyal retainer, had spirited away the treasure buried with him. After a while, people probably came to forget who had been laid under that barrow so many years before.

Today I'm on my way to the class I'm auditing at the University of Alaska. Students like me are hurrying to and from classes of their own. While the university has made its best effort at keeping the sidewalks cleared, we people have worn in our own preferred paths through the snow. Though these paths are rough and wobbly, they are often more direct than the ones the university has provided. People are like that.

I am thinking of a line from a poem by Robert Penn Warren that contains this admonishment: "We must learn to live in the world." When I read them, those words jumped off the page at me like a punch in the nose. *Must* learn, the man says, as if living doesn't just happen, but is an act of conscious will. For some people it must needs be so.

What does just happen is death. The famous suicidologist Edwin Shneidman used to say that dying is the one thing we don't have to do for ourselves; death will happen for us. I suppose he fed his troubled patients this nugget of what you might call wisdom to keep them from taking death into their own hands. I wonder how often he was successful.

This past week a man named Nick Hughes, a man I slightly knew, killed himself. Whenever I hear of such deaths, I think, *Yes, we must live in the world, but how is it we learn?*

What I knew best about Nick Hughes was that he sure could ride a bike. That's how I met him, cycling with a bunch of guys, mostly scientists, from the university and town. Chasing him up a hill, I would find myself frantically downshifting. *When,* I wondered, *would he shift to the small chain ring?* Most of the time he would not, bulling his way up the hill in an exceptionally high gear, leaving me and most of the others to catch up if we could.

Nick Hughes's death made me read a book by Calvin Trillin, *Remembering Denny,* a book that came out in the '90s, a book I had been meaning to read for some time. This fellow Denny was Trillin's college friend at Yale, a guy so full of energy and magnetic charm that Trillin was not the only one who imagined him as a future American president. Denny killed himself instead.

Like Trillin, I am the son of a grocer. Like Trillin, I came from a household where college was an expectation, a great expectation I would say, since neither of my parents had attended college and saw college as a golden doorway into the future. My mom, not my dad, was the driving wheel of this ambition. She valued education for its own sake. Having finished high school, she briefly went back as a graduate to study Latin. What would the value of Latin be for a girl working as a clerk in a general merchandise store? Love learning, she seemed to think, and vocation would follow. Her only wish for my brother and me was that we "amount to something."

Until now, I've never appreciated how open-ended that indefinite pronoun made my life. Unlike a good number of the guys I went to college with, I had my parents' blessing to do almost anything. For a short while, my prospects looked a little dim. After graduation, I worked at a basketball camp, saved all my money, flew off to Europe for a less-than-grand tour. When I came home, I took a job in a foam rubber factory, loud, dangerously fumy, low-paying. By summer I had applications in for high-school teaching positions, but was painting houses. Still, I was reading; I'd always been a reader. "That's all right," my mom said, "as long as you're using your education." How, though, could she not have been disappointed?

That life I briefly led is what Calvin Trillin means by "the provisional life." Now in my fifties, I see the children of my friends often leading such lives, moving from one part-time or seasonal job to another. Spending freely or maybe putting by enough to travel to an exotic place. There they will spend freely, too, but their dollars will stretch further.

What is the nature of their ambition, and what is the nature of my own? How do we come to know if our ambition is too great or too small? Is there any ambition that meets the Goldilocks standard of "just right"? (It's worth remembering that Goldilocks comes to know "just right" only by repeated trial and error.) Nick Hughes's parents were Ted Hughes and Sylvia Plath. Some of his friends didn't know who these famous poets were; others knew but left it alone. I knew but never let on. When I was introduced to him as a member of the English faculty, I felt him draw back.

Nick Hughes's death makes me wonder about the kinds of ambition people have. His parents didn't just want to be good poets (they were, each in very different ways, good poets), but recognized as good poets. From their famous first encounter, which resulted in Plath biting Ted Hughes on the cheek, it was clear they were ambitious in a fiercely competitive way.

Somewhere right now, a pretty good poet is writing a pretty good poem, maybe even a remarkably good poem. Maybe it will climb out of the slush pile of a pretty good literary magazine and get published. Maybe somebody, maybe dozens of somebodies will read it. For me, a writer of prose, not poetry, that small coterie of attentive readers would be enough. Why is that enough for some, and why is it not for others?

Poets, pretty much all writers, are not going to be recognized as they walk along an airport concourse. At this station of life, I have to wonder who would want to be. Who would assiduously court a sort of fame that could never be turned off? Who could live a life in which he might be famous but at the price of never being left to be merely himself?

Trillin writes about the slots we find ourselves fitting into. Trillin himself finds his way into journalism. It's a comfortable fit as his career has proved. But his friend Denny, known to his postgraduate colleagues as Roger, never seems to find what seems to be his foreordained slot. What if you don't?

After Sylvia Plath's death, Ted Hughes's ambition to be a well-regarded poet must have been knocked off its expected course. From then on, he would be known as the estranged husband of the poet who killed herself. Nobody can guess how this deflection affected him on his path as a writer. Just the same he persisted, he wrote more poems. Different poems than he might have written otherwise, but some good ones.

When my grandfather came to this country at the turn of the twentieth century, I imagine he had made a decision to leap from his circumscribed existence in the Old Country to something better. He had already tried other things. He had been a hussar in the Austro-Hungarian army. I'd like to think he had an adventuresome spirit. When he allowed himself to be recruited by a representative from an American company to go to work in a coal mine, he may have discovered that he had traded one set of constraints for another. For his sons it would be different. When World War II came along, my dad enlisted in the navy. Jumped, maybe, before he was pushed into the army. Unlike his older brother Joe who was shot up on the beach at Anzio and came home damaged physically and psychologically, my dad came home alive with fresh possibilities. My grandfather died two weeks before I was born. I grew into a world he made for me.

What happens on a group bike ride is that riders form a pace line, each rider taking a turn at the front, the others trailing in a long tail. As long as a rider can maintain his place in line, the riding is easy. At the front, the leader is working pretty hard, while back in the line people may actually be coasting. Once a rider falls out of that protected slipstream by only a few feet, it's very difficult to get back in. Cyclists call this "getting dropped."

Sunday, after a bike ride wherein I was quickly dropped from the pack of serious riders, I found myself pedaling along with two men my own age who talked about their daughters' schoolwork and their college ambitions. Then I went home and sat on my porch and began to read both the Anchorage and the Fairbanks papers from front to back, as I always do on Sunday. In the warm spring sun, I pulled off my bike jersey and a while later pulled off my shorts and sat on my porch naked reading the paper. Though I didn't think it at the time, I can say that at that moment, as at almost any moment in my adult life, I was as free from the con-straints felt by my father, my grandfather—by, most likely, every ancestor I could imagine back to the time when we had no clothes to wear—as a person could possibly be.

I was and am rich in days, rich in time and possibilities. The question is how to use the days we have. For the Greeks, the Stoics, the idea was to accept with equanimity the good and the bad, to roll with the punches as my mom might have told us, her version of *amor fati*.

Just the same, I've often felt I have lived a life on the verge of getting dropped. My poor grades at a good college were barely enough to get me into graduate school before the wave of grade inflation hit. I was able to find an instructor's job at a good uni-versity during an economic downturn, a downturn in which pro-fessorships were being reduced to instructorships. I was able to publish just enough to find a job as an assistant professor at the school where I most wanted to be, and to publish just enough to get through the tenure gate. An incredible string of luck, all to land me in a slot I was happy to occupy.

As for others: I knew a guy from college. He was among the few premeds in my class who did not get accepted into a medical school. What he found instead was a job teaching high-school biology, a job he hated before he even began. I knew some men I taught with at another university who were denied tenure. They went to what was then called a PhD retread program and became loan officers in banks, middle managers in nondescript companies. For all of them, the lives they prepared for themselves were not going to happen. When the world we've been encouraged to imagine ourselves a part of won't have us, then what?

My parents' grocery store was a dying business in a dying town. Eventually, it failed as it must. What did my father feel the day he hung the lock on the door for the last time? He was no longer who he had been, who everybody had grown to expect him to be.

Is this what Germans call *weltschmerz*, world sickness, a kind of sickness we must all get a touch of at one time or another? I wonder if it isn't something like bird flu or swine flu or one of the many other viruses that sweep the world. Some people get a bad case; some hardly feel it at all. From time to time all of us must have a touch of *weltschmerz*, a lost job, a divorce. Most of us get over it; for some few it's fatal.

When I was crazy for a while, I told the psychologist I felt like a fish in an aquarium. Probably not an original analogy, probably one she heard once a week. Things happened to me that caused me to hit the glass, caused me to be aware of the glass that had been there all along. That is still there. After being less crazy for a while, I am less aware of the glass. Out of view most of the time are certain hard limits. One such limit would be the span of my life.

Mustn't every day be a recalibration? I think of what we might call the story of my life, constantly under revision. Here's a day, a day on the Copper River dipnetting for salmon. As I drive to the river, I imagine myself getting my limit of thirty fish in a matter of a couple of hours. After a while, fruitlessly sweeping my net through the water, I begin to concoct a wholly different narrative starting from the other end . . . the story of my getting skunked. I have never been skunked dipnetting at Chitina—yet. So the narrative I have in my head as I begin my drive home is a story of a more or less successful trip. My life, so far at least, has been like that. More or less successful, some days more, some days less.

As free as I imagine I might be while sitting out on my porch naked, I am not. I could make a simple test but need not. Anybody could guess what would happen if I took off for town. Fairbanks, all of Alaska, is a very tolerant place. I could probably make it down my road naked, even make a fair distance along the main road before the state trooper some thoughtful person had called would arrive to take me in.

Everybody has a list of those we know who've killed themselves. Mine begins with a high-school classmate who drank antifreeze (not the best choice), a college classmate who shot himself, a graduate-school classmate (his method unknown to me). The fathers of my good friends from high school, college, grad school. I think of those grown men often because they killed themselves at a time of life near my own, a time when maybe they were too overwhelmed by disappointments. At least that's what I've told myself.

I think of Native kids in Alaskan villages, where suicide among the young is a plague. I think of suicide bombers. I think of soldiers who have survived months of duty among suicide bombers only to come home and kill themselves. For each suicide I have sought something close to a causal explanation. Because of this, then that. I know it's not so. People weather disappointments in love, in work, in the lives of their children every day and manage to survive them, manage often to overcome them.

Nick Hughes was a well-regarded ichthyologist, a fish biologist. On the few times I was able to keep up with him on his bike, we talked fish and fishing. He wanted to find places where he could shoot good pictures of grayling from within the clear water they prefer. I wanted to keep wild trout in a fish tank in my home. We both seemed to want to participate fully in this world.

Mr. Shneidman, the suicidologist, thought suicides live in a swirl of emotions too complicated for any of us on the outside to sort out. Considering the outcome, I have to think, too complicated for their suicidal selves. Theirs is a Gordian solution.

• • •

What my mother meant when she charged my brother and me to amount to something was for us to do anything except fail.

I think of Samuel Beckett, as I often do, of his heroes (I was about to say antiheroes, but it seems to me that survival in Beckett's world is a form of heroism, maybe the only true heroism). Who could ever have been so thoroughly put into a slot not of his making than the Unnamable, armless, legless, stuffed into a bartop urn people use as an ashtray? Yet as he famously says from his urn, "I can't go on, I'll go on." Go on. What else is there?

My father took up a life of volunteering, a life of doing for others. My mom hung his certificate of appreciation from the governor on the wall beside pictures of my brother and me graduating from college.

In *Worstward Ho*, Beckett does offer another solution: "Fail better." I like that one. There are at least two ways to consider it for a motto. One is to measure the self against itself. Every day contains hundreds of ways we fall away from our own initial expectations, beginning from the minute we get out of bed and find the socks we'd hoped to wear in the dirty clothes hamper, the first of many small disappointments to be overcome.

The other is to measure the evidence of our many failings before the audience of the world. When my graduate schoolmate killed himself, I was baffled, somewhat grieved (I didn't know him that well). He had recently failed his comprehensive exam. His major professor, my good friend and a Beckett scholar, was angered. That man was a long-distance runner, a finisher of marathons even if it meant walking.

Psychologists say we remember slights and insults better than compliments. My own memory tells me this is so. Do we remember our failures better than our successes, too? Is there a point at which all the slights, disappointments, and failures (real and imagined) fill the brain to the point that the best of our memories are driven out? A point where the idea of failing better seems a bad joke on us?

I'm not sure how many, if any, of his fellow cyclists knew Nick Hughes suffered from depression. I didn't. To see him on his bike was to see him at his best. Climbing Chena Ridge above Fairbanks, he and another biologist had pulled away from me and an oceanographer. Still in hollering distance, I hollered for them to wait. As they did, Nick turned his bike back and forth in long, looping arcs. A moment of unalloyed joy to clip and save. And not enough.

I realize I am a finisher, too. But I cannot tell whether I finish because I would hold the failure against myself or whether I would be ashamed. To put myself before the world, to wear a number and set out on a course, is to set out to fail better. Every mile—every step, actually—is most often a falling away from the expectation I began with. Judged by the world or by myself, eventually I must be dropped.

Here is how my father spent the last day of his life. He watched a college basketball game on TV when he wasn't dozing. When he learned the last name of his nurse, he tried to figure out whether she might be related to people with the same last name in our hometown. This is the man he was. This is how he chose to live out his life. He went on. At some point he and my mom had agreed he would not allow the doctors to attach him to the ventilator machine again. He would go on, but only on terms of his choosing. At last, when night came, he dozed off and didn't wake up. When my time comes, I hope I can do as well.

Dead Animals I Have Known

Driving up the Parks Highway toward Fairbanks and home, I hit a red squirrel. It darted out from the side of the road and did the usual indecisive red-squirrel dance, racing to the left and then the right as I braked hard but not hard enough to skid. Nonetheless, I hit it. In the rearview mirror I saw it flop and twitch and finally lie still in the road, dying the way we used to play at dying when we played army in the woods.

Just as easily I could have missed it. It could have managed to run into the other lane, run back into the brush on the shoulder, or frozen as I straddled it—what must be imagined as a near-death experience for a squirrel. But none of those things happened. I hit it and it died.

Less than a mile later, I hit another one in the same way. I wanted to pull over, but my wife, Margot, said, "It wasn't your fault." If not, whose fault was it?

I have eaten more than my share of meat. My grandfather was a butcher, and he taught my father the craft. By the time I was a boy, though, it was illegal to dress an animal in my father's retail butcher shop, so sides of pork and beef came in through the back door and were hung on meat hooks in the walk-in cooler. I can't remember a time when I wasn't used to seeing animals in pieces. Just the same, I've never intentionally killed a mammal.

Margot and I were on our way home, having spent the past ten days in Denali National Park hanging out with the animals. Once, walking along the park road, we came upon a boar bear grazing about seventy-five yards off. We were easing by when one of the park buses came along. It pulled to a stop and all its passengers rushed to the starboard side to get a better look at the bear. Margot asked the driver if we might come aboard. "Ma'am, that bear's not interested in you," the driver promised her in a lilting Irish accent. And he told her he would come to the rescue and pick us up if the bear started for us.

Instead, as we got farther around the curve in the road, the bear got wind of us, rose up on his hind legs, and squinted at us. It seemed to take him a moment to decide what we might be, and once he did, he dropped back down on all fours and set off at a run in the opposite direction.

In the park, set down among the animals, we have been reminded that we are more like them than not. Not so much as the predators you might think, but as weak, slow animals that rely on cleverness and treachery to maintain our grip on the top rung of the ladder where we are clearly not alone. Out in the park, we are exposed.

In this moment with the bear, we'd come closest to the encounter Margot had both sought and dreaded. Every day she had imagined opening our cabin door and seeing a wolf or a bear, or better still a lynx or a wolverine, on the path to the outhouse. But we'd seen only Arctic ground squirrels, hares, and magpies around the cabin. The ground squirrels were especially cheeky, climbing up on the porch to lounge and sun themselves, growing more comfortable with our presence by the day.

Up on the ridge, we could sometimes see a bald eagle going to roost. Surely each of these squirrels would be a tasty morsel. In fact, the squirrel I came to imagine as the patriarch of his little tribe bore scars along his back that suggested he'd made a lucky escape from some predator or another.

My friend Janis told me once, "No animal wants to die." She was talking about her cat, "a little sleeping nodule," content to pass its days balled up on a towel under a high-intensity lamp. A good life, you might call it. One day it might be lucky enough to go to sleep and not wake up. But it had to go to the vet instead.

· · ·

Early one morning as I drove on the way to a group bike ride, I flushed a flock of sparrows from the roadside. One bumped against the windshield, its wings beating, its clawed feet scrabbling against the glass as it slid up and away over the rooftop. I would like to believe it flew off to join the others, but even though I didn't see it fall to the road behind me, I know it couldn't have survived the encounter. I've never intentionally killed a bird, either.

I put back most of the fish I catch. Usually I can easily slip a barbless dry fly out of its jaw without lifting the fish fully from the water. If a barbed hook gets too complicatedly embedded, I'll snip it off.

A biologist friend in Virginia took bluegills that had swallowed hooks home with him and put them in an aquarium to see what happened. Nothing he could see. They lived on, and he eventually took them back to the lake where he caught them.

We call this kind of fishing sporting. By sporting I mean we have made up rules, made a sort of order for the whole world. All the other animals have no real say, but they must play along. Janis once asked me, "What kind of guy drags his friends around by their lips?"

Walt Whitman said he would rather turn and live with animals. I know the feeling, wanting to be free of the crazy guilt that makes us human, the hierarchies, the rules, the notion that some god is watching over us all.

Here is how my friend Kes saw a small wolf pack take down a caribou in the park, take it down in the East Branch of the Toklat right near the cabin we stayed in. The wolves drove the caribou into a channel of the glacial river and lay down to wait until the caribou couldn't stand the cold anymore and came out. They chased it back in. This time it stood in the cold a shorter time, and when it came out, the wolves again chased it back. It was a big, healthy bull caribou, not a weak cull from the herd. When the wolves were confident the caribou stepping out of the river was too weak to fight them and too tired to run away, they took it down. The kill was quick and efficient, and so was their feast.

Out on the deck, our own cat is batting at the glass door. A red-backed vole hangs limply out of her mouth. Margot sees it and hollers, both angry and distressed. The cat, Fatty, you would think too slow to catch anything. But there it is. "Don't let her in!" Margot tells me. We don't, and the cat turns her back to us, sits crushing the vole in her jaws. The sound of a cat eating a vole is like that of a person eating a crispy pickle. She eats it all except for a red blood spoor left on the threshold.

This is what animals do.

• ◆ •

Even those people driving around with "Eat more moose—12,000 wolves can't be wrong" bumper stickers admire wolves at the same time they resent them. I doubt if a wolf has any such conflicted feelings about us.

I saw a lone wolf in Denali National Park once, trotting along the park road. Our bus driver said it had been part of a pack that had taken down a moose. But in the struggle, it had gotten its ribs kicked in and, now weakened, it had lost its position in the pack and was out on its own. Skinny, frail, the wolf glanced over at the passing bus. Its eyes said it all: it was not our dog and never would be our dog.

Which is too bad for him. We humans spend a lot of time thinking of ways to eliminate the other animals on our rung of the ladder. And thinking of ways to eliminate the animals we regard as pests or superfluous. Red squirrels are the most common roadkill in this state. Unlike me, some people don't regret hitting them.

Once outside Circle Hot Springs, in midwinter, I skied toward a cabin along the shore of Medicine Lake. From a distance, a strange fringe appeared along the bottom of its walls. When I got close enough, I saw the fringe was made of red squirrel tails nailed about six inches apart. How many must there have been? Dozens, a hundred, a couple of hundred? The fringe ringed the cabin, presumably as a warning to other red squirrels to stay away. A person could see how well this had worked.

Still, I understand the impulse. One summer when I had been away for a while, a red squirrel gnawed a hole through a three-quarter-inch piece of plywood under my house and pulled the insulation out, replacing it with close to a peck of cached mushrooms. I can't remember exactly what I thought as I was pulling all those mushrooms out of that hole, but it was probably something like, *The little sumbitch.*

I got a live trap from Fish and Game, baited it with a peanut butter cracker, and caught the thing (him? her?). And I put it in my truck, hauled it down to the university, and let it go on the ski trail behind one of the science buildings. My neighbor, a biologist, told me the squirrel probably beat me back home.

So when I saw the squirrel or one just like him out on the porch rail chowing down on bird seed, I thought, *Well, maybe this would be the time to pop him with a pellet gun or a twenty-two.* I don't own a gun. It turns out I'm cross-dominant, right-handed and left-eyed. My eye doctor says I'll never shoot straight.

When we build our homes in the woods as we Alaskans like to do, we build them in places where animals already have homes of their own. We like the idea of having them around, up to a point. The lone wolf who has lately been spotted on our road is a good example.

Even those of us who belong to the Sierra Club and the Audubon Society and contribute to the World Wildlife Fund are looking for some kind of dominion over beasts and birds. Regardless of whether we believe our dominion is a divine gift or something we just have claimed for ourselves, we exercise it every day of our lives.

◆　◆　◆

Remember when I said earlier I'd never intentionally killed a mammal? I forgot one. When I was a seventh or eighth grader, my friends and I found a kitten badly mauled by a dog. We wondered what to do and, practical boy that I was, I picked up a cinderblock and slammed it down on the kitten. We buried the kitten and went on with our boys' lives. I didn't tell my folks; I doubt my friends told theirs either. Really, what else was there to do?

Before Margot and I went to the park, we checked out a bear safety video from Fish and Game. In the movie, a woman allows a grizzly bear to false-charge her several times. The narrator warns us again and again not to run from the bear but to stand our ground and talk to the bear in a commanding voice.

But Fish and Game officers usually load their twelve-gauge shotguns as follows: two whistler rounds, a couple of rounds of heavy buckshot, and then the rest of the magazine full of lead slugs. I've fished a day or two with a borrowed shotgun loaded with slugs on my back. Considering my previously noted skills with guns, it was at best a silly gesture, and it wasn't much fun.

On the other hand, I've fixed the bird feeders so squirrels cannot raid them, but just now outside the window I can see a red squirrel on the ground under the feeder vacuuming up all the spilled seed.

I said I hadn't intentionally killed any birds either. It turns out I disremembered about that, too. I thought about it the other day when I was reading a book wherein people ate squab and thought them delicious. The summer before my sophomore year in college, I had a job painting company stores. Mostly inside, but once we were asked to paint the outside area of the Pocahontas Company Store. There, tucked away under the eaves, was a pigeon's nest with fledglings in it. It had to go, the store manager told us, and we were to make it go. It was easier than you might think because pigeons keep both an untidy and a nasty nest—sticks scattered everywhere and guano running down the walls. So I can't work up much enthusiasm for eating dead pigeons by any name.

All us painters held the pigeons in contempt, the way most of us do all animals that have come over to our side. Would that be the dark side? Would that be our dominion?

Remember the squirrels dead on the highway? In my list of ways they might have lived I pretty much suggested that with a little more gumption, they might have saved themselves. I didn't say what I could have said: I could have driven more slowly. I could have not driven at all. Really. Except I'm not going to do those things. Probably, reader, neither are you unless you are a practicing Jain, a sect reverential of all life forms down to mosquitoes and those fiercely determined biting bugs we Alaskans call white socks and so having virtually no followers in Alaska—or anywhere else in the United States, for that matter.

◆ ◆ ◆

Down on the Copper River dipnetting, I catch a red salmon, haul it to the bank, and gather the net around it so it can't escape. It thrashes wildly until I get it settled on a big flat rock, pick up my bonking stick, and whack it hard right above its eyes. If I'm lucky, one good bonk does it. The fish shivers from head to tail and that's the end of it. Other times, it squirms this way and that and I don't make a clean hit. I have to hit again and again. Sometimes its eyes pop out. Always a trail of blood and slime begins to ooze out of its gills before I can get it on my string.

Once I had lined up my fish on a fairly flat spot by the river and was gutting them one by one when they began to slide slowly down and into the river. Three or four got away. Sickening. They were food. They had gone to waste.

At dinner one night, our friend Nate, a commercial fisherman and hunter, explains to Margot the moment when an animal changes into a piece of meat. Once a deer has been shot, it transforms into a different kind of problem; the solution, he says, is to cut it into shapes people can eat.

Sometimes I fantasize about all of Fairbanks bringing their freezer-burned salmon, moose, and caribou meat and piling it up in the Fred Meyer supermarket parking lot. *How high would that mountain grow?* I wonder, while these thoughts all bob around together inside my head:

José Ortega y Gasset says every hunter should kill with regret, and when he does not, it's time to quit.

Native people say to kill with respect and gratitude.

It turns out that a diet rich in protein and fat is good for an active person. Anybody who lives in the north could tell you that.

I have learned not to look a caught fish in the eye, the eye that darts around in panic seeing nothing at all familiar in its range. A fish doesn't need words to know what's coming.

Each in our own way, we do what we can, what we must, what we will.

I'll willingly trade some of my fish for moose meat or caribou.

Why Is It That We Do This?

Things they do look awful cold . . . Hope I die before I get old.

—Pete Townshend

In a previous life, I was a high-school track coach, not a very good one. At a triangular meet at a nearby school, a meet held in a hard, steady rain, I stood outside officiating and soaked to the skin in my teacher's clothes while the boys huddled on the school bus, coming out only when they heard the third and final call for their event. By the time of the next-to-last event, the two-mile run, the cinder track was a sodden mess. My two-miler came out, shivering in his skimpy uniform, and as he made his way to the starting line he said to me, "Tell me again why it is we do this."

I could not answer him then and have been trying to answer, if only for myself, over the forty-odd years that have passed.

My grandfather was a pick-and-shovel coal miner; my other grandfather was a butcher. Each in his own way did physically demanding work. I doubt either felt any need to get out and go for a run or a swim after work. Sport was for the leisure class. And men who got their physiques from working out (think of Jay Gatsby exercising with his Indian clubs) were looked down on. Real muscles came from doing real work.

Except: Weren't people then, as now, starstruck by feats of athleticism? Haven't grown men always read the sports page first? And like Achilles, many of us must have had at least a fleeting ambition for lasting fame, for lifting ourselves above ordinary mortals. Sport was the most apparent way and so perhaps became the fuel for our daydreams.

Some years ago, my pal Musgrave and I were cycling up the hill to our houses, up Spinach Creek hill in Fairbanks, steep and longish. I said, "What are we going to do when we can't do this anymore?" "Play checkers, I guess," Musgrave said.

No kidding, though—what? As we grow slower, as we travel shorter distances, how do we come to terms with who we are, who we were, and who we are becoming? Is there a better question to ask any person who persists in running, skiing, cycling, or playing any sport when almost everybody else his age has taken to his couch to watch people on TV do better the thing he tried to do in a younger life? How lasting is lasting fame, anyway?

We are mere mortals. And lasting fame? I read recently of the death of Fiorenza Magni, an Italian cyclist from the 1950s. While he never won the Tour de France, he did win the Giro d'Italia a couple of times, and finished second in his last Giro in 1956 despite weather bad enough to cause sixty other riders to drop out, and while riding with two broken bones. Remember him?

Records are set only to be broken. When Roger Bannister broke the four-minute-mile barrier, his achievement, his record, did not last through the following summer. And how many times has that record been broken since? I cannot say what it is or who holds it now.

As W. B. Yeats would have it, far better to think of ourselves as souls fastened to dying animals—with heavy emphasis on the soul. "Caught in that sensual music all neglect / Monuments of unageing intellect." That's it in a nutshell. When we are eating or having sex or just sitting by the fire enjoying its warmth, we ought to be thinking higher thoughts, or at least thinking. Our bodies would be mere husks, vessels supporting a higher mind. We don't properly know who we are because our animal selves ("sick with desire") keep getting in the way of our more lofty selves.

Would it be trivial to make the observation that exercise is said to be good for you? Though some say it can be addictive. Addiction might be understood as when the body gets a hold over the mind. Whether it's a simple matter of chemical dependency—drug addiction, say—or this: addiction to the supposed endorphins, our very own chemicals, which our bodies produce during extended exercise. Our bodies rule our minds. Can it ever be otherwise?

"Feel like a healthy animal," a '60s ad for Special K breakfast cereal proclaimed. A rampant polar bear in full roar is juxtaposed beside a male human tennis player in a similar posture—plus tennis racket. Pictured below are a bowl of Special K, a pitcher of milk, a glass of orange juice (small), and a cup of black coffee. Just what a polar bear or any other healthy animal would want for breakfast.

My cavil with the ad, actually pretty progressive for the time, is with the simile. "*Like* a healthy animal"? Why not "Be a healthy animal"?

A guy named Brian Jay Stanley has written about this very thing, his anxiety over having a body. Not only is the thing physically disgusting, "I resent how matter lords it over mind." When I read his op-ed "I Am Not This Body" in the *New York Times* I felt sorry for this man, felt pity that he was missing so much of the fun of being an animal. We *are* our bodies. We are, I would add, in this moment living as much as dying animals. Though when we die, we will be returned to inert matter. If there is a difference between us and the other animals, it's that we know the truth of our mortality all too well.

I watch the cat as she rolls onto her side and pulls herself along the carpeted stair, as she races frantically through the house for no clear reason. At a friend's house, I watch his son, not yet one year old, trying to roll over, just as he will soon try to sit up, crawl, and walk. The cat may have no self other than her sensual self. She plays to please herself. But is "please" the word? Does she do what she does because she must? Does the child will himself to roll over because of a deep biological imperative? How far will that same imperative push him? And why does it seem to push some of us further than others?

It usually hurts to be tackled by another football player. Running a race like the four hundred meters can only make for searing pain in the runner's lungs and legs. Even fit athletes throw up after arduous runs or swims or skis. So it is that most of us just quit all that nonsense.

Those who are true athletes are encouraged to continue; in fact they seldom know when to quit, and like Michael Jordan or Johnny Unitas have to be ignominiously eased from the roster. Jocks, though, some of whom might be athletes, but need not be, play on. But for different reasons.

Isn't there something crazy and prehensile about all this jock stuff? Yes, we're animals, yet we've spent our whole evolution trying not to be, and a fair amount of intellectual energy convincing ourselves we are something other than. Who wants to sleep on the ground, out in the rain, go hungry, sleepless, get sick, and die? Maybe Brian Jay Stanley is right. Wouldn't I rather be a big brain bathed in a tank of stimulating nutrients thinking timeless thoughts like some creature in a sci-fi movie?

A female friend once told me she always thought of me as a big boy. Meaning, I suppose, that she thinks of me at play—skiing or cycling or gone off fishing. And maybe, on top of that, being less than earnest about what she imagines life's more serious undertakings to be. But what she might think of as play, I would call a joyful endeavor, a spiritual practice, a means to the discovery of a few thoughts that the rest of the population might think of as worthwhile.

I have something of an answer for my runner's question now: what's in it for me. But really, that's just another question.

I put aside basketball for a long while, and when last I stepped on to a court found I could barely touch the rim—I, a guy who could dunk off a half-step, I, a guy who could touch the top of the square with both hands, had grown earthbound. For a brief moment, I had a notion to begin a regime of leg presses, rope jumping, and plain old jumping, the sort of jumping I indulged in all the time as a kid—touching awnings, grabbing bunches of leaves from low-hanging branches—but I let that impulse pass.

Here's William Wordsworth in an aside addressed almost to his private self in "Tintern Abbey": "The coarser pleasures of my boyish days, / And their glad animal movements all gone by." Yes, his vertical jump has left him, but he and his sister Dorothy have walked out to see the ruins just the same. They famously walked all over the English Lake District. Some pleasures give over to others as our muscle mass decreases.

The range of our sensual possibilities is as great as we allow it to be. To slide swimming through the water, to throw myself into a wave and ride it until it rolls over me and grinds me to the sandy bottom, drags me along, and spits me out. To crank up a long grade on my bike, pleased to crest the summit and to have earned the glide down. To find my rhythm in a cross-country ski and feel I can go on forever until suddenly I realize I can't. To realize the can and the can't are part of the same package. Every workout, they say, is a good workout. Some are good just because they are over.

I was glad to stop playing football. Practice for a lineman is tedious; and, as I've said, banging against other players hurts. Yet a couple of days ago, the first day the air turned sharp and crisp, I found myself thinking nostalgically of football practice: the smell of the grass, the feel of the cool air in my lungs making me feel I could run forever. I even remembered the joy of colliding with another player, the simple animal joy of having a body and putting it to use.

In Alan Sillitoe's story "The Loneliness of the Long-Distance Runner," the narrator, Smith, speaks of the joys of running, of being the first man and the last man on earth. It is his one time free of the tedium and control of his keepers at the Borstal. Running is his release into himself. Yet because he has something of a gift, he becomes the boy his supervisors pin their hopes on. Smith will carry the day in the cross-country race against boys from other Borstals. Smith is leading the race until he comes into view of the spectators; then he begins to walk, allowing a kid from another

Borstal to best him. As he would have it, this is the only way to be true to himself, and maybe true to the private joy of long-distance running. It may be the best moment in sports writing I know to illustrate what it might cost to own yourself fully.

When I began skiing fifty-kilometer events in my forties, finishing one under three hours seemed possible. With the right weather, the right snow conditions, fitness level at its peak, and no nagging injuries, maybe I could do it. I never did. My last 50K took me four and three-quarters hours. I chose classic technique rather than skate skiing, which is faster on warm snow. I had a nagging muscle pull in my back. I had missed a good chunk of training and one preparatory race because of the flu. So I had my excuses. Except I thought, and continue to think, that I should still be able to get back under four hours. With the right weather, and so on. I keep slipping down the ladder; I keep trying.

My old running buddy from Blacksburg, Tom, writes that he's looking at 7:40 mile splits in his distance races these days. Tom, who was always faster than me at a time when knocking down consecutive sub-six-minute miles seemed no trouble at all for either of us.

How do people know their limits? Do we find them or are they forced upon us? This marks my seventeenth year of skiing Sunday mornings with SCUM, Sugai's Class of Uncoachable Men. When we began, most of us were in our forties, a few in our late thirties. Now we are in our fifties and sixties. We persist. But among my fellow SCUM, some of us have hit barriers, barriers hidden in our DNA that have suddenly revealed themselves. What happens when our hearts or brains or knees or hips or ankles will not let us do what we would ask them to do? This isn't about going slower, but about not being able to go at all. Who are we then?

When we compete in an individual event, we are all essentially alone. A friend, a teammate may be by your side, but how can he know what's in your head, how much lactic acid has started to build up in your quadriceps? How might he gauge your level of confidence, your growing doubts?

Sometimes people ask me to explain why I find long solo bike trips so satisfying. To take a trip where everything—food, clothing, shelter—is contained in the panniers of my bike, to have myself as my only motor is to return me to my true self. Every hill has to be climbed, every route navigated, every mechanical problem solved. Every problem is my problem alone, every success mine. There are fewer variables, fewer people and events standing between me and who I am. Last summer I found myself pushing my bike up a hill. It wasn't the steepness of that particular hill but the number of such steep hills that had finally worn me down. So I pushed. I could not remember pushing up a hill since 1977 on another solo tour. But really, what else was there to do? The animal's solution—get on as best you can.

Years ago, I saw a picture of a crane in full mating ritual in *National Geographic*. The light from behind its outstretched wings showed its biceps, puny as marbles. Not so different from my own. I have tried to find joy in my animal self, and to live with that animal self: too skinny, too tall, clumsy, not blessed with a lot of fast-twitch muscle. No amount of working out with Indian clubs or free weights or weight machines was ever going to make me build great muscle mass. I would have to make do with what I had. Thinking of my own skinny arms, I felt a kinship to that bird, far flyer, symbol of long life—how much could be accomplished with so little.

I cannot stop myself from getting out and living through my body. There is always the recognition, cutting through the satisfaction of doing well or the disappointment of doing poorly, having pushed myself to my limit or beyond it, that after a little rest I will come to see I'll do it again.

Why is it, then, that I do this? I still can't say—pleasure comes in many forms, many of them irrational—but I am sure I can do nothing other than hope to continue, getting slower and slower until finally I blink out.

Driving Directions to
the Homes of the Dead

Scrawled on a rumpled sheet from a legal pad:

US 29 into US 501 ~~South~~*—North*
Graves Mill Road—Exit 11
Left on Graves Mill/VA 126 1.6 mi
Left onto US 221 1.3 mi
Left onto Bateman Bridge
Left onto Homestead
Rt onto Oak Knob
Lt onto Crestline

The house at 113 Crestline is a small, ordinary bungalow on a street of others just like it. Once it was the home of Herb Francisco, though I have no idea who lives there now.

Herb was the guy our coach called the most natural athlete he had ever coached. Herb knew in his bones the many ways to dodge and feint on a basketball court, on a football field. He was relentless and unafraid to take a hit and give one. Herb should have already died many times over. In Vietnam, where he was the sole survivor of an ambush on his patrol. In a body with a congenital heart condition that killed his dad when Herb was still a toddler. From the diabetes that dogged him for decades. It's remarkable, then, that he made it to age sixty-two before he did die.

I could drive over to Forest, Virginia, and see who lives in Herb's house now. Or starting from Witten's Fort, and driving up into Poor Valley, I could come to the brick house on a piece of pastureland. Porter Murphy's house. Or the big white house in Pound where Porter's sister, Sharon, lived before moving to Atlanta. I have the quickly written addresses and directions to them both. Porter and Sharon no longer live in those places, or anywhere else.

Once we put the dead in graveyards. They stayed there, and we went to see them. When I was a boy my aunts still made regular trips to the cemetery where their parents, my grandparents, were buried. My paternal grandfather died before I was born; my grandmother died when I was three or four. I barely remember her, a distant woman in her Old Country bib apron trimmed in rickrack toddling down the boardwalk beside her house. Or did I get that image from a photograph? My aunts took me along to the cemetery to place flowers in the vases built into my grandparents' gravesites. Our visits, then, were a shared expectation.

Nothing new here: people have been tending the graves of loved ones since we lived in caves. Maybe they thought the soul of a dead person would linger nearby. Maybe they thought an appropriate sense of reverence would be achieved when near the last resting place of the dead. Or maybe they thought, as so many of the living have thought over the centuries, that having not given their loved ones their due when they were alive, they could make it up to them once they were dead.

At different times, people have formalized grave visitation. The first Decoration Day was in 1868 when people placed remembrances on the graves of twenty thousand Union and Confederate soldiers buried at Arlington National Cemetery. This official day to remember the dead morphed into Memorial Day, a three-day weekend, the semiofficial start of summer and an occasion for commercial enterprise.

As if to read my thoughts, my brother has written to say that if I can find a buyer for the burial plots our parents bought for themselves, I am welcome to the money. The local paper offers half a dozen ads for such plots; it turns out they might be worth a good bit.

I try to imagine what would make going to a gravesite more significant than just thinking of a loved one wherever a person may be: solemnity? But what if the dead hadn't been a particularly solemn person? Herb Francisco dressing out for football practice, pulling a jockstrap over his head, yelling, "Hey, y'all, look at this: a Chinese nose guard."

I picture my aunts bustling in their kitchen with a coal cook stove, pecking at each other over details of the meals in the lilting eastern European accents they never managed to shed. Stuffing some bills into my hand, saying, "Buy yourself something," all of us recognizing I'd grown away from whatever they might imagine I'd want or need. Herb, Porter, Sharon: I might find them in the halls of our school, in the gym, on the ball field.

The Pocahontas graveyard, now fallen into disrepair, was once a place where courting couples would walk among the dead. There were benches placed here and there; there was a fishpond filled each summer with goldfish. And there were the graves of the many inhabitants who'd gone before us—coal miners—many, many of those. Tombstones speaking of the ethnic mix of this place—stones inscribed in alphabets and languages few visitors these days can decipher or read; graves of Hungarians, Italians, Poles, African Americans among the original white folk settlers of the place—certainly more dead than living in Pocahontas now. I can't remember a time when it was otherwise. Cameo photographs of the dead were placed under glass ovals on many of the tombstones; almost all have been taken by souvenir hunters. It couldn't matter to the dead, and probably not to their descendants, now scattered far and wide. In what way do these photographs of people not known matter to the vandals who took them?

I have no idea where my mother's mother was buried. If my mother visited that grave, well away from Pocahontas, she had stopped by the time I was born.

Down in the fruit cellar, cleaning out my parents' house so it might be sold, I found some old stiff ribbons and some calling cards—cards I figured out had been attached to the floral arrangements from a funeral, my grandmother's funeral. I had never known her, never known much about her, and—selfishly—never thought to ask. This much I did know: when my mother was thirteen, a terrible age for a girl to lose her mother, her mother died of uterine cancer. Until I found those ribbons and cards, I had never thought much about how this event affected my mom. I know there had been trips to Baltimore, Maryland, for radiation treatments—which at the time would have been powerfully and indiscriminately applied. My mom: the baby of the family and the only girl in a family of four brothers. Her dad: a cranky and taciturn German.

My grandfather's job disappeared when the company he worked for went bankrupt in 1936, down in the bottom of the Depression. The family decamped from Fairmont, West Virginia, to Pocahontas, Virginia. Through that move, through three subsequent moves to the house I grew up in, my mother had carried these ribbons and cards along. They lay in the basement, emblem of a little knot in my mother's heart—the one memento, as near as I could tell, of that hard time. Put away, but not thrown away.

The next time my brother and I talk by phone, we try to recall exactly where my parents' unused burial plots are located, and from there we begin to wonder about the whereabouts of my aunt Rosie, aunt Barbie, cousin Louis, uncle Joe, and our grandparents on both sides. I cannot recall where the gravesites I was taken to as a small boy are located. I am tempted to Google "my dead relatives" and imagine finding pin drops across a map indicating sites in Virginia and West Virginia. We do know none is buried in the Pocahontas cemetery, though it's only now I've thought to wonder why.

Joe DiMaggio put flowers on the grave of Marilyn Monroe for twenty years after her death. And then he stopped. And my aunts gradually stopped their Sunday visitations to the graveyard, too. Did the dead suddenly grow distant from those places? Did the living outlive their grief, or did they find another place for it? Judging from appearances, a few of the more recent graves in the Pocahontas cemetery are still attended. A few people still come to the graveyard looking to commune with the dead.

And I try to picture Herb among flowers, little flags, a marble monument. I imagine him looking around to see if anybody is watching, and then unzipping and marking his spot. That would be Herb.

◆ ◆ ◆

Where do most of us go nowadays when we go looking for the dead?

The first mummy I ever saw was in Basel, Switzerland. I was bumming around Europe; it was a Sunday and I couldn't think of anything to do except visit the small nearby museum. There it was, all unwrapped and about the size I was in fourth grade. Recognizable as a crudely formed human being, but that's about it. Not at all like my uncle Joe in his casket. Not at all like my mom when her heart stopped, her blood stopped circulating, and the color drained from her face. A dead person with no place left to be except in this hermetically sealed glass case.

Just outside Charlottesville, Virginia, is an experimental station run by the Virginia Department of Transportation. There, cadavers are placed in cars, crashed into other cars with a cadaver at the wheel, and inspected for damage. I think of my dad when I pass by. My dad had hoped to give his body to be used by a medical student at the University of Virginia, where he had been treated and cured of cancer the first time around. These days, though, once a person donates his corpse to the state he has no say in how it might be used or how it might be disposed of. Once it has served its purpose, the remains are cremated. We have no idea where my dad's ashes went.

Surely we carry our memories of the dead with us wherever we go. Surely we bump into moments when those dead seem as alive in our thoughts as they ever were in their corporeal form. I catch a glimpse of a smug high-school jock in a shopping mall and see Herb's lazy slouching walk, thrown-open varsity jacket, loafers with no socks, a Lucky Strike in his mouth. His two last-second shots rimming out in the Whitewood game. His best game and we lost. I could go to that gym and still mark the two places where he took those short shots. I think his teammates could, too.

When I pull down a pan taken from my parents' kitchen, I see my dad making a batch of cookies. Somebody has taken a picture of me, reading the paper, my glasses slipped down on my nose; I am the very image of him, down to my watching a televised ball game with ironic dispassion. Or my mom's chair she sat in at her sewing machine, whipping out aprons for Christmas presents, now in the Maine house. I hear her singing badly and enthusiastically in church, speaking her mind with passion at our kitchen table.

Right now, in one of the storage spaces in our place in Maine, a portion of my mother's ashes lies waiting to be scattered. She visited that house once, and I think she enjoyed her visit. Among her mementos of that visit was a refrigerator magnet in the form of a tiny lobster boat. I took it from her refrigerator, cycled it back to its place of origin, stuck it on the refrigerator in Maine.

*　*　*

Maybe a grave might be a monument to ourselves, a token of our standing in the world. In the Pocahontas graveyard stands the McGee crypt, a substantial structure, maybe six feet high and eight by ten feet, with a peaked stone roof. Legend had it that one of the McGees was interred with a ruby ring on his finger—or her finger. Somebody believed it enough to chip a hole in the roof. Through that hole in broad daylight a person could see a compromised lead coffin and the bones within.

As a boy I never knew any McGees, and I wonder how they might have felt knowing that this monument to their family had been reduced to a cool site for Halloween visitations.

It was Christopher Wren's children who placed the words "If you seek his monument, look around you" on his marker in St. Paul's. Maybe Wren felt that way, too; he thought his work on that building was his finest. It could be this is the rare example of the monument and the man becoming congruent.

Genghis Khan, I think, had a better idea. Nobody knows where he is buried. He wanted it that way. The slaves who dug his grave were killed by his soldiers who, in turn, were killed by other soldiers. Then a river was redirected to flow over the gravesite. For centuries people have crawled all over the Asian steppes looking for the place. In this way the khan made his presence felt better than any monument he could have erected. His son, though—a weak ruler and a drunk—ordered a massive tomb built for himself.

Recently I heard an account on the radio of a woman forced to flee her home as a forest fire approached. She carried a loved one's ashes as she went, saying she wanted to make sure these were the real human remains and not what was left of her couch. I'm not sure how it matters.

Regardless of whether my parents meant to, they seem to have followed the khan's example. I think of my dad's long-gone ashes, and my mom's. To scatter hers here and there is just a way to confirm what I believe—memories of her inhabit these various places in my thoughts, leaping out at unexpected moments to surprise me.

As they should, all the better to return us to more complete, more complicated memories of the dead. Herb as a ball player, all sinew and muscle, as a man late in life with a belly hanging over his belt, and a multitude of Herbs in between. Herb was a player of cruel practical jokes. He and another ball player pushed an older guy, a not-right guy who'd kind of become our school's mascot, out into the snow as he tried to make his way—naked—to the shower. He bound and gagged a teammate with athletic tape and left him on the backseat of the darkened bus on the ride back from an away game. Luckily, the bus driver discovered the guy as he was parking the bus. There are worse stunts, too. I won't tell those, but I won't forget them, either. Without them, without my remembering them, Herb would not be Herb but a sanitized and, I would say, diminished guy.

Despite my skepticism of the whole graveyard proposition, after my parents died I readily joined with my brother in putting a monument to them in the Pocahontas graveyard. Neither of us has visited the site since we placed and dedicated the stone, placed it on a steep pitch overlooking the town. We had their names and the spans of their lives inscribed on the slab, along with this epitaph: "They will always live in Pocahontas."

What was it we thought we were saying? Maybe that here in this small town tumbling to ruin, more than any of the other places on this earth, is where my brother and I cannot take a step without thinking of them. And it would be my hope that those coming on the marker would think of them, too. Or, not knowing them at all, these strangers would wonder, Who? Who would care so much for this place, whose whole identity would be so tangled up in its day-to-dayness as to linger here even in death? Finally, not too many generations later, wonderment will be all that's left, the same sense of wonder a person might feel looking for cognates to serve as clues to those buried under the stones inscribed in Hungarian. Just a wish to know who lived in this place, and why.

Should you be curious enough to go there:

Driving west on US 460, take the exit for VA State route 102.

Follow Route 102 through Bluefield, Virginia, to the old N&W underpass. It flooded down there anytime there was heavy rain. And beyond, just on the other side: that's where a guy trying to get to Pocahontas stood to thumb a ride.

Notice the improved Norfolk Southern bridge. It doesn't flood there anymore, but there are fewer trains.

Route 102 is a narrow road, poorly maintained with steep drops to the shoulder. We drove it fast and fearlessly; I think I could drive it blindfolded today. Pass in and out of Virginia and West Virginia.

Pass through Falls Mills; look up the road to a lake behind the old N&W dam where my dad (mostly) took us fishing, where my mom (mostly) took us swimming.

Yards, the holding area for all the coal cars waiting to go into McDowell County to be filled. Once there were many, now none.

Nemours, where my mom's dear friend Mim lived until she moved. Slow to make friends, Mom would never have a friend that close the rest of her life.

Wolfe, where I filled pop bottles with water from the creek and handed them up to my dad to feed into the radiator of the overheating Divco truck.

Stroupsville, home of the poorest of the poor. Their yards full of interesting junk, their lives in their shacks a mystery beyond me.

All just wide spots in the road, as my mother would have had it. People lived there just the same, among them our customers.

Cross the meander we called Laurel Creek—full of minnows in the spring and summer despite the coal-dirt creek bed—and start up the hill. Note the drywall, over half a mile long. Though it has been damaged and poorly repaired, it remains a marvel. Look.

Beyond the wall, see the sunken mass grave of the 112 miners killed in a single blast. Take in the listing and fallen stones. And the few newer markers, my parents' among them.

Look across the hill to where the old school, my parents' school, my brother's, and mine, stood, now an empty gravel lot.

Cross the asphalt bump where the railroad tracks once ran before they were pulled up.

Snake past the abandoned gas station and car wash.

Pass the train station that became the dairy bar, and is now a secondhand store and charity where used clothes can be had by the needy.

Pass the closed beer joint, said to be the roughest bar in the coalfields in its day. Pass the empty storefronts, their cast-iron facades brought in on the train, once thought to be a rarity. My parents' store, collapsed roof and back wall, is among them. Then go around the courthouse and the wide place in the road where we kids played Indian rubber, batting a twenty-five-cent rubber ball until put out by a ball caught on the fly or on first bounce, playing in the street despite the traffic. Pass the coffin shop, perhaps this town's most opportune business. You're in Butts Hollow now. My mother called it Spruce Hill.

Last house on the left, uphill side. A duplex, but a good, solid brick house. They lived a good life there. We all did.

As for me, that graveyard marker is a kind of lodestone, pulling me back. Of the places in the world I could go to, that I do go to in my head, those I wish to visit, those I cannot avoid, this is the road I find myself traveling most often, tracing every turn until I arrive.

Some Fibbers

I went to school with this kid, Charlie Ray. He was a big fibber. He told wild fibs of his athletic prowess, the toys he owned, his influential family. When kids called him on them, he didn't back down, but told even bigger fibs.

To tell the truth, it's hard not to fib. I believe all of us have built an internal notion of who we are, and there must come a time when our internal selves and external reality don't square. We are not as smart or fast or skillful as we imagined ourselves to be. Or maybe as we imagine we should be. Had circumstances not conspired against us, we would have, could have.

Maybe that was what Dr. Frederick Cook was thinking when he made his false claim at the beginning of the twentieth century to have climbed to the summit of Denali, the tallest mountain on the North American continent. It was an era when exploration of the more distant parts of the earth was in fashion, when explorers were the heroes of the day. Cook had made trips with Robert Peary to the Arctic and had been along on another trip to Antarctica. While neither of these trips achieved the goal of reaching the poles, Dr. Cook acquitted himself well in his professional capacity. He is credited with saving the lives of many crew members, among them Roald Amundsen, on the Antarctic expedition when the *Belgica* became ice-bound.

So why fib about the Denali climb? Perhaps so Dr. Cook might, like Achilles, gain lasting fame.

It's worth remembering that Patroclus dies wearing Achilles's armor. His death, just like his hero's, is an act of hubris. But for Patroclus it's not excessive violence, though his day in battle wearing Achilles's armor is bloody enough. He has achieved a moment of glory by temporarily taking on the identity of another man. When he cannot let it go, can't shed his secondhand glory and quit the battle, he is doomed. Regardless of whether Patroclus deserves glory (when Hector kills him, he surely must know the man he is fighting with is not Achilles), he claims it. His is a need, almost an addiction, that drives an ambition for renown in the eyes of the world.

Maybe it's our fault, too, our need to find a hero out there to admire. When Lance Armstrong began his skein of seven straight wins in the Tour de France, people rushed to him: more than a mere cancer survivor, rather a survivor who rose to the top of an incredibly difficult athletic competition. And our need to find him admirable made almost everybody willing to overlook or explain away the implausibility of his feats. Lance, some said, had benefited from more scientific training methods than the cyclists who'd come before him. He had good teammates and a good coach.

Frederick Cook was a founding member of the New York–based Explorers Club. After his Denali climb, and before it was discredited, he set off on a second major expedition to reach the North Pole. The wind was at his back, as any explorer of his day might have put it.

We all have a tendency to build a version of ourselves that does not necessarily represent who we are. I'm thinking of J. M. Synge's play *The Playboy of the Western World*, in which a young runaway turns up in a not-so-far-off Irish village (it is a small island, after all) and dazzles the locals with his tales of derring-do, augmented perhaps by his easy charm and good looks.

Harmless enough, I suppose. And Alaska has been a place where just such transformations might take place. A guy could come here, and as popular folklore suggested, simply start over with a new identity, even a new Social Security number, and become a whole new man. And if you could talk your way into a job and do it, well, good on you. We might even imagine this to be evidence of a person's true self making its way into the world.

I told a fib a little while back. A young woman asked me if I had played college basketball. (It was a watershed in my life when the verb in that question went from *play* to *played*.) When asked simply if I played basketball, the answer is a simple yes. I played a lot; I lived my life around basketball as a high-school boy. And for a variety of complicated reasons, I did not play in college—a choice that I regretted. Maybe I still regret it. But I didn't play, so when this young woman asked and I said I had, I fibbed.

Possibly this was the same sort of fib that Frederick Cook indulged in: under another set of circumstances, it would have been true. If the weather had cooperated better, say. So let's just say I could have played on my college's freshman team. I think I could have. But I didn't.

Sissela Bok, in *Lying: Moral Choice in Public and Private Life*, says every lie we tell pokes a hole in the social contract. I picture that contract written maybe on parchment or vellum and displayed in a climate-controlled glass case like the Declaration of Independence or the Constitution. If every lie is a perforation, our contract is in tatters. Because Sissela Bok means every lie, even the ones we tell for seemingly good reasons, the white lies we tell when our spouse asks if her new haircut looks good, say, and we want to be affirmative. Or lies that use words to soften criticism.

Maybe she is right, but possibly some people value kindness more than a hard truth. Both might carry moral weight, so how to judge? But lies of self-aggrandizement belong in another category. Fish get bigger. Hikes more arduous. SAT scores go up, maybe job titles and salaries do, too.

And so does the temptation to make what we wish were true, true in our telling. The biblical injunction against "false witness" seems to me addressed to lies that are directly damaging to others. So the self-serving lies we might tell would hurt only the tellers. In some essential way, this is true.

A bunch of other guys climbed Denali a few short years after Cook didn't, the Sourdough Expedition. Three strapping young guys and a somewhat older leader started up the mountain from the north side, and one day under ideal conditions, the three younger ones made a successful dash to the summit. For fuel, they carried only a bag of doughnuts and a thermos of hot chocolate. They also claimed to have carried a fourteen-foot spruce pole, which they erected on the top to prove they'd made their climb. Okay, when it turned out they'd climbed the slightly shorter north peak of Denali, they never pretended otherwise.

What interests me is the fourth guy, the older expedition leader who stayed behind at the base camp. As the young climbers received more acclaim, this man, Tom Lloyd, began to adjust the story until he had finally talked himself onto the north summit along with the other men.

Maybe we are all capable of this sort of willed disremembering. An old colleague of mine told me a story of a bunch of guys he'd gone to high school with getting drunk at a bonfire, driving in an old VW bug down a steep hill, and winding up fetched up against a tombstone at the bottom. Over the years, another classmate, a guy who'd been standing by the fire when the drunken partiers had stumbled back up the hill to tell their story, has remembered himself into that runaway car. Small potatoes, nothing to shift the fabric of history. But does that man truly remember himself in the car, or does he know every time he tells this anecdote that he's fibbing?

There is a certain school of thought, among southerners especially, that values a tale well told over the facts of a matter. I spent an afternoon with the writer Barry Hannah, and he, drunk as a skunk, told me stories of flying F-4's off the *USS Bonhomme Richard*, of tuning in to the Chinese opera on his airplane's radio set. All lies, all elements made into his character Quadberry from his best short story, "Testimony of Pilot." When I complained to my thesis adviser about these fibs, he just said, "He expected you to tell a good one back." But if you do too much of that entertaining misrepresentation, don't you lose sight of the actual? I always thought so, feared it would be so.

Part of this worry is tied up with the obligation to remember people and events clearly. Part is recognizing that errors will occur no matter how hard I try to get things right. So I try hard.

And Charlie Ray? Guys picked on Charlie Ray; we called him "Mayonnaise." Today people would say we bullied him. He was a fat little guy, spongy as a marshmallow, and capable of running a stream of provoking blab that would annoy any kid and most adults. When he did, guys—even mild-mannered guys like me—hauled off and hit him. From there it got to be a kind of sport to get him worked up into a panicked rage, to hear his sputtered invective. Guys held him down and gave him red bellies. A couple of older guys made him give them blow jobs.

Charlie Ray moved away. I forgot about him; probably we all did. Then he was back, a grown man, cooking at the nearby Holiday Inn, and still telling his whoppers. A local newspaper reporter was taken in. There he was in his cooking clothes under the big headline "Chef Charlie Ray." And in that story I read of his many decorations from his service in Vietnam, his history of cooking in some of the best-known kitchens in the South, and, most impressive of all, his friendship with the late Princess Diana. He produced a small set of royal salt-and-pepper shakers, a gift from the princess.

That basketball lie was not the worst lie I have ever told. It's an example, though, an example of how the world at some point offers a chance to tell a lie and get away with it. And being six-six and all, I have had that chance many times before. Why did I take it that once? I can remember the where and the when. I was in the Fish and Game office here in Fairbanks, getting my lifetime fishing license all Alaskans over sixty are eligible to receive. And a young woman at the counter asked me about the basketball and I fibbed. Fibbed about an event that didn't happen more than forty years before.

All the people I'm writing about here, Frederick Cook, Charlie Ray, Lance, me, would all like the world to see us as larger than we really are. As long as we can think straight, though, the gap between what we claim and who we are must only grow wider. The cognitive dissonance for somebody like Charlie Ray must have grown huge over the years. But would it be any different for Lance Armstrong? How does a person go on?

In other words, "What does it profit a man to gain the world and lose his own soul?" That's Jesus talking, chewing out Peter for thinking too much of a person's standing in the world. And it's like Jesus, or like the way the writers of the New Testament present him, to move the question beyond simply telling lies to everybody else, to telling them to ourselves. Self-aggrandizement comes to be a hollowing out of the self, making a person into a kind of chocolate Easter bunny, nothing there except an inviting outside.

Frederick Cook submitted a claim that he had reached the North Pole. Unfortunately, his described route had a remarkable resemblance to the route of the fictional explorers in Jules Verne's novel *The English at the North Pole*. It seems likely that Cook did not reach the North Pole, though he could have come very close. And Admiral Peary made a concerted effort to ensure that the world knew he got there first. Peary, too, might have missed the mark, might have done a little fibbing himself. But once Cook's climbing partner, Ed Barrill, signed an affidavit testifying that Cook's claim of the Denali summit had been faked, Cook's credibility was forever compromised.

What were his old pals at the Explorers Club saying about him just then? And what could Cook say about that photo he had contrived to have taken of him standing on a craggy summit? Even if Belmore Browne had not found Fake Peak and posed there himself, another explorer would surely sooner rather than later reach the true summit of Denali, where the pictures alone would tell the tale. Getting found out was the only possible outcome for Cook.

Browne had made several goes at the Denali summit himself. Perhaps the most admirable aspect of Browne's attempts was his honest admission that on two successive days, he and a climbing partner had been turned back just yards from the summit by high winds. Then again, having established himself as a great debunker, how could he do otherwise?

Lance Armstrong's fibs are another level of magnitude, though. I imagine Cook after having spent considerable amounts of money, after suffering the bugs and the cold and a certain amount of rotten luck, wishing he could get to the top of that mountain. His decision, I want to believe, was a spur-of-the-moment thing.

In the records of the Tour de France, the titles of Lance Armstrong's seven races have simply been vacated. So many other cyclists were doping during that time that no true winner of the race could be determined. But before we excuse Lance on the grounds of "everybody's doing it," it's necessary to remember that the other competitors seemingly acted independently. Lance organized what has fairly been called a syndicate involving teammates, doctors, support crew, and even the team masseuse—all acting at his behest and for his benefit. All acting under a cloud of financial dependency and threats.

Dr. Cook moved to Texas and got into the oil business. When he sent out a prospectus offering spectacular returns on an investment in his oil well, he was prosecuted and convicted of mail fraud. The well, it turned out, was successful, paying out even more on investments than his prospectus had promised. Lance Armstrong is being pursued by a pack of lawyers representing former sponsors and teammates, including a major witness against him, that opportunistic doper Floyd Landis. Landis's own Tour title has been vacated.

As for Charlie Ray, there are Vietnam veterans who make it their business to expose false claimants of Purple Hearts and Bronze Stars. They called him out quickly enough; he'd never served, much less been decorated. From there his phony cooking

152   UNPLEASANTRIES

résumé was easily discredited. The fibs about Princess Di went without saying. A short time later, Charlie Ray killed himself.

The next time I slipped into the Fish and Game office to pick up a dip net permit, I was greatly relieved that the young woman I'd fibbed to was no longer with the office. She had moved on; with luck she has forgotten our encounter.

When compared to lies of consequence—say, our government's lies about Vietnam or those nonexistent weapons of mass destruction—none of these fibs has any great moment in the history of the world. In 1913 Hudson Stuck would lead a group of men to the top of Denali. Probably only a handful of climbers and Alaskans know his name. And I doubt many people could name another winner of the Tour de France, even that other American, Greg LeMond. Except for a few schoolmates and an embarrassed small-town reporter, Charlie Ray's story will be considered only by the few readers of this essay. And most likely forgotten by them soon enough.

Admitting a fib is harder than telling it. The cost of a public and grand-scale fib is enormous. But the cost of little undiscovered fibs is just as great. We lose sight of who we are; we become exhausted by the necessity of keeping our false narratives inflated. I can understand how Charlie Ray could not continue to live that way. When we make such choices, we don't fully understand how hard it will be to unmake them.

I hear there is a group of people who believe Cook did climb Denali, and they go around giving talks to defend his reputation. There are still people wearing the yellow rubber-band bracelet of Armstrong's Livestrong Foundation. In the future there may be a group going around giving talks defending Lance. We do need our heroes.

Sometimes regret can save us, not the regret that prompted fibs in the first place, but the regret found in the recognition of our own self-destructive egos. Mistakes cannot be unmade. Like the corrections in a newspaper article, the true story can never fully replace the fib. More knowing, but not necessarily wiser, I do what I can.

No Place Like

I once liked nothing better than taking long trips on my bicycle. To have all of one's needs strapped to such a skinny machine had its appeal. To ride all day and exchange fewer than a dozen words with other people. To sit by my tent in the evening and read until darkness came. My bicycle came to contain its own small ideal of order defined by my two safety-orange panniers and my brown canvas front-end bag-of-many-pockets. Inside my left pannier I carried my Svea cook stove nestled inside a cook pot and a shallow pan; wrapped around them all was my tube tent, my home, scarcely more than a plastic tarp and mosquito netting held together by Velcro, ties, and a long zipper. In my right pannier I kept my few clothes. Outside pouches held spare inner tubes, white gas, bits of cord. My front-end bag held my tools, maps, water bottle, books, and notebooks. A headlight doubled as a flashlight. My poncho covered me while I rode, covered my bike while I slept. Unpacking these few things in the evening and repacking them in the morning became a small ritual, a celebration of my self-reliance, of my wanderer's soul.

My father, a home-loving soul, was born in Pocahontas, Virginia, in 1921, in a neighborhood of white board-and-batten company houses called Maple Grove, though probably more often called Hunk Town. The house still stands. My aunt Helen and John Sabo still live down there, the last two Hungarians in Hunk Town. When my father married my mom, Pocahontas was still booming. Housing was tight; he moved in with her and her father in an apartment above a storefront. Several years later, they moved around the corner to the Little House, not a little house at all, but long, tall, and skinny and named for the people who owned it. Sometimes people called it the long house. The first memories I have of actually inhabiting a house come from there. I played soldiers outside in the little dirt patch next to the steps with Ronnie Baker, the kid who lived in the back half of the house. Our enemies always had to be Reds; I had no idea why. I went to sleep when my mom turned off my lamp with cowboys on its shade and a wooden stirrup for its base. I marveled at the stained glass window that let light into the room where the new TV was. And I remember riding in the back of my dad's truck with a load of our things as we left that house and moved a little farther around the bend to the top of Butts Hollow into a tall brick duplex.

My former wife took a picture of me standing in front of the only house I have ever owned just after we closed on it. I am tilting off to one side and am pulling the pocket of a pair of khaki pants inside out, a kind of joke against a mortgage, the kind of debt that could keep me awake at night until I finally settled into it, the way a person might settle into a minor physical discomfort, an achy knee joint, say. (Isn't life a constant settling into such discomforts?) When my wife and I moved in, our cats were so disoriented that, even though we were sleeping right there in the room with them, they tried to dig their way through the carpet and escape under the door.

The cats got used to the house and the expanse of woods quickly enough. And I did, too. I once declared I wanted to die in that house when my time came. And I meant it. That house was open and airy, with lots of south-facing windows and a living room with an expansive wood floor that opened into the kitchen. There were cats; there were comfortable chairs and many cups of tea. There were decks you could pace to help you toward clarity in your thinking, decks you could sit on absolutely naked if that's what you cared to do. There was a garage where I could work on my bicycles and wax my skis, make clumsy things out of wood.

Like all houses, it had enough wrong with it, plenty of what Realtors call "nonconforming features," but so do I, and that may have been part of what made me grow to feel at ease in it. That Spinach Creek house stands outside Fairbanks, Alaska, sheltered by stands of aspen and birch in what locals call "wilderburb."

At that time, all the way across the continent, my mother still lived in the uphill side of what was once our new brick house. The Elletts lived on the other side. When my dad was a twelve-year-old boy, one of the Ellett brothers—Mr. Aubrey, I think it was—came out the double doors of their general merchandise store and asked, "Which of you boys would like to earn a quarter stocking shelves?" After that, my father was very nearly folded into the large Ellett family. He worked in their store, delivered groceries by horse and wagon and later by truck, and learned to drive on an Ellett vehicle. He did chores in their home, became a fixture in a corner of their kitchen. Later he would drive the young Ellett men to dances in Blacksburg and beyond—until the war broke out.

And as he was so enfolded, he must have grown away from his own family. Down in Maple Grove, a person could get along speaking only Hungarian. Every summer the kids went to Hunkie school against the day when everybody would quit the coalfields and go back to the Old Country, back home, and live like kings. It might have been the war, or the events of 1956 that put an end to this talk of going back, but I guess it was the kids themselves. The Pochick boys bought cars and souped them up; my father skipped school and hitched rides to Bluefield to watch baseball games. He played football. He graduated from high school and settled into work.

My father didn't wish for much in this life, and what he did wish for he kept to himself. But he wished for this, though, his last wish, important enough to wish aloud: to die at home. He was disappointed. It's hard to die at home these days unless death sneaks up on you. And in his case it didn't; it came from a long way off.

In my mom's basement, recently flooded, she had brought up from the mud our old baseball gloves, a collection of school papers that went back to my brother's and my grade-school days and on into high school, her own accumulated materials from her days as a Cub Scout den mother when this basement room was our den, as well as the pine cones, milkweed pods, and acorns for her Christmas wreath projects. In that mix were also the cardboard flats that had held the cans of condensed milkshake-like food my dad took through a tube in his stomach and the small box of the horse syringes we used to push his meds through the same tube. Not grisly, not morbid, not even sentimental, it was just stuff, just information, accumulated sometimes intentionally, sometimes happenstantially, about where we have come from and where we are bound.

Who can say where we will come out except that it most likely won't be where we wished to go? At least it seems that way to me. I believe my dad wished for as much as anybody; he just couldn't render up his wishes for the rest of us. What he offered us instead were these: that he would go off and live in Tahiti, that he would own a Cadillac. Playful wishes of exotic comings and goings and the barge that might carry him along.

Instead, my dad and mom climbed all the way up the hill to live beside one of the men who owned the store where they'd both once worked, where they started courting. Instead, they bought a store of their own and had two small boys.

Our side of the house had belonged to Mr. Junius and his wife, Mary Babour. The yard was designed for contemplation. A dozen goldfish swam under the water lilies in the two fishponds, upper and lower, connected by a stone and concrete canal. A clearwater spring fed them both. Flower beds, some planted with perennials, some needing replanting with annuals every spring, made giant steps up the hillside. A slender path wandered through the denser woods where concrete toadstools waited in private nooks. Just in time, couples might come upon a wooden loveseat with trellised roses climbing all around it. At the very top of the hill stood a large, open summerhouse with two stone fireplaces fitted with griddles for cooking out. In the lower yard was a playhouse just for kids.

My brother and I made short work of all that. We stamped through the flowers while floating our boats in the fishponds and managed to fall in every now and then, too. We dug rocks from the terraced walls in search of lizards and salamanders, ran along the paths using sticks for spears. We knocked baseballs through the windows, played the yard down to a dusty strip. When we saw a new toy called a Slip'n'Slide advertised on TV, we got the idea. But having no long plastic sheet, we just turned on the hose until we made a muddy river and slid down it like otters along with all the other kids on the hill.

Inside, my brother and I invented a game called knee football for wet winter days. You scuttled along on your knees and were not considered tackled until your head had been banged to the floor. The chandelier in the dining room swayed, the china cabinet chimed its crystalline rattle. We busted the stuffing out of hassocks by turning them on their sides and riding them down like horses. One year we pulled over the Christmas tree while wrestling around. The Elletts' children—daughters—were my parents' age, grown and gone. The Elletts themselves, Mr. Frank and Brownie, were stoic and uncomplaining. Mr. Frank wore a hearing aid.

The war must have been enough for my dad to settle any restiveness in his bones. Across the great Pacific he saw exotic islands, open ocean, ruin and death. I picture him up early, four in the morning, getting breakfast together for the ship's crew. Joseph Conrad knew sailors are the most provincial of men. Their ships are rolling and heaving homes, the sea a constant, if untrustworthy, neighbor. When they make landfall, a quick turn ashore is usually enough, and then back aboard, back to what they know. At home in a galley just as he would later be at home in a kitchen, in a butcher shop, a cup of coffee near to hand, my dad was up early preparing the day for everybody else.

Other men (mostly they were men) felt compelled to set out. Usually, they set out for the West. The most extreme of these men, the mountain men, simply wandered. They seemed to have had no ambitions to find gold, or furs, or good land for crops or cattle, or to open trails for the more reliable types who would later follow. They just had to go, to get away from the rest of us. Some, as *The Way West*'s author A. B. Guthrie would have it, were what we might call sociopaths, too violent, too unstable to be around others anyway. So they wandered through the West, across the plains and into the Rockies and even down into California. Though the mountains seemed to be what they preferred.

Thoughts of home must have fallen away as they went. Years would pass before they might happen to return. Like Rip Van Winkle, they would have found their towns had changed, the old home place in different hands, their kin having moved on or simply disappeared. Nobody was waiting for them unless it was in the graveyard.

Yet doesn't there remain a romantic draw, a secret wish, in nearly everyone to wester? To drift? To search out some new place?

When I started off on my own small cycling trips, I would imagine a long umbilical cord spooling out behind me, connecting me to those I loved, finally leading back to my parents' brick house on top of the hill. And I would think—with all respect for simple physical comforts—that this need to be connected was what was most unlike anything the mountain men seemed to want for themselves. After a few days' travel, I recognized that I, too, was growing disconnected. Routes, weather, the geography of the moment were all that mattered. But didn't the going out always take longer than the coming home?

Ours was a four-sided family unit. On one side of the kitchen table, my mom and me, on the other, my brother and dad. Always at the same places, fixed as a constellation. Until the time came for me to leave for college. My mother found an enormous footlocker in the old apartment above the store, painted it red, and stocked it with all the supplies she thought I needed—pencils, pens, paper clips, notebooks, stapler, hole punch. The pencils and pens bore the advertisements of the salesmen who'd given them to my parents as parting gifts for me. Filled with piles of clothes and bedding and blankets, our front bedroom became a staging area for a long, arduous expedition. When the day came, we loaded the car and set off. My brother, left behind for school and football practice, stayed in the kitchen, washed the breakfast dishes, and cried. He was right to; something had been sprung loose that could not be put back. Three years later, he set out on his own similar journey.

In *A Woman's Story*, Annie Ernaux tells about going away to school, about how a university education was her mother's greatest wish for her daughter. Yet she could not foresee that this wish when it came to pass would be the undoing of their special relationship. Soon enough Plato and Aristotle and all the rest came to stand between mother and child. While the mother felt a vague and terrible sense of loss, what her daughter understood was how irrevocable this distance, arrived at through new ideas and experiences, must be. Back at home in the flesh, she could never quite be home again.

Insofar as we can, we carry our houses on our backs. Maybe what we have is a pickup-load of stuff, or a trunkload, or just a shoeboxful. When these odd things are around us, wherever we are must be home. My digs as a young, single high-school teacher, as a graduate student, as a beginning instructor of college English, all had the same transient feel. They were filled with an odd conjunction of many of the same objects: elegantly made serigraphs and lithographs; a library table painted over with green porch paint I used for my desk; a lamp that was an uncle's old shop project and resembled a bowling pin affixed to a hubcap; a couple of small wooden crates I used for dictionary stands and bedside bookshelves; a grungy yellow plastic cup, my rinse-after-brushing cup, a cup perhaps with me since my college days.

After six months in a hospital, after climbing up out of pneumonia and sliding back into it again and again, after being too weak to walk and very nearly having to learn how all over again, my dad got to go home. When he left, we carried several bags of his accumulated possessions to the car. These were pajamas, slippers, and bathrobes. Things he'd never worn at home before. But now home would be different. He would remain an invalid; our dining room would become his sickroom.

On the drive he declared to me, "When I get home I'm going to walk up our steps and hug your momma's neck." And by this he meant alone, on his own power. We had practiced in the hospital mounting thirteen stairs, the number from the first floor to the second and our bathroom. The six to the front porch would be easy. And so I hung back and let him, let him be true to his word.

At the end of my bicycle sojourns, I came to crave the *idea* of home. I wanted nothing more than to sink back into its familiarity. To be warm and dry with no sleeping bag, no tent, no temperamental camp stove. I wanted the newspaper box just down the driveway; I wanted refrigeration. Home is, after all, the place you have to come back to, the place where they have to take you in.

The trouble is, things won't stay the same. On the morning of his first full day home, my dad got up and took a shower, shaved, and led me to the kitchen. We were going to bake shiny-top cobbler. Like a jazz musician too long away from his horn, my dad was eager to get his chops back. On his instructions I pulled out all the ingredients, but by then he was running out of steam. He sat on my mom's paint-spattered kitchen stool and directed me through the recipe off the top of his head. At one point you might have thought he goofed, but good jazz musicians don't goof, they just improvise. The cobbler turned out fine, but as the days passed, my dad grew too tired to try baking again.

One day when I was learning I could not live in my house in Spinach Creek anymore, I went onto the roof and started pulling wads of leaves out of the gutters. It was the short Alaskan fall; the job had to be done before they became frozen in snow and ice. Then I took up a broom and started sweeping the decks. When I got done, when I got things caught up, put in order for winter, I thought I could leave this big house for her. But when my wife came out and asked me what I was doing, I couldn't tell her. I started crying instead, and I stayed on six more months.

When my father died, I was still in Alaskan air space, somewhere between Anchorage and the Southeast Panhandle. The call had come from my brother that morning, and it had triggered a series of calls to travel agents, colleagues, and friends. My last phone call to Dad had been garbled and confused. It wasn't the best connection. "Call back later, okay?" Dad had said, because he was tired. Maybe, probably, he knew he was dying better than his family could. If I had known, what would I have told him?

Sometimes I think this is what we might wish for the most: that there be emotional ties, stronger than physics, geography, mere biology, that hold us to our loved ones. When they feel pain, we should be pierced by empathetic twinges; when they feel grief, we, too, should feel a wave of inexplicable sadness. And when they pass from this world, some unspeakable gulf must open within us, never to be filled again. So across continents and oceans, even, we would be in touch, we would know.

What I could not tell my wife was how I had come to feel imprisoned in our house, sometimes held prisoner by love and goodwill and what they asked of me—that I try to live in a shape I could not maintain. It is very nearly impossible for me to drive back to Spinach Creek, to see the house standing above the road like a great riverboat, as my wife liked to say. How she manages there I cannot say, cannot imagine except that I know a little about how a person can put up with a lot when there seems to be no other choice. Or when the need for a home is strong enough to overcome all else.

After a short stop in a small green cabin, a lifeline from a friend, a place so cramped that I later heard it called the "Unabomber cabin," I have fetched up in my current cabin, spacious and luxurious by Alaskan standards. Sixteen by thirty with two full floors and a Monitor heater, it too has windows that look to the south and a deck (though both windows and deck are smaller). And in it are the wooden crates, the ugly lamp, the serigraphs and lithographs looking just as unlikely here as in my other quarters. So are a sofa bed and a leather reclining chair, furniture so redolent of me that my former wife could not bear their presence. I fetched them away after getting insistent notes that they must go, and go quickly. For a good while, small bits of flotsam regularly turned up in my departmental mailbox, appeared in grocery sacks hung from my office doorknob, as she tried to rid the house completely of me, as she tried to remake it into a home.

There is a moment in *A Clockwork Orange* when Alex and his droogs, driving a stolen car, approach a sumptuous house with a cleverly lit sign at the end of the drive announcing "Home." By the time they have done with their vandalism, torture, and rape, they will have ensured that this house will never be a home again.

It must be clear that I do not wish to stay in this cabin the rest of my days, that this is a cozy place for a single guy and a small cat. The cat is most at home here; she celebrates the steep stair, the many built-in shelves and crannies, the wide windowsills for sunning on winter days. She owns the weedy yard and dedicates herself to keeping it free from squirrels and voles and even nervy dogs. Yet when I leave it, I know I will grieve it as much as she will, that to be uprooted again will be hard on us both.

I made a disordered retreat from Spinach Creek, summoning all my strength, hardening my heart and locating dozens of boxes at the liquor stores around town for my books. The clothes I just dumped on top of the load. I took my fishing rods, my bicycles, my skis and tools. I took the things that most defined me. I left debris. I left like a coward when my wife was away, thinking maybe there would be less pain for both of us that way. My dad could have warned me; I should have seen the warning in his dying year. There is no lessening of pain.

In the divorce proceedings I learned that regardless of the quality of one's home furnishings, they have no real monetary value. Everybody's stuff is junk in the eyes of the court. Yet my stuff—my junk—had held me in the orbit of Spinach Creek for a long time. Even the yellow plastic cup had come to serve as part of my sense of who I was and am (for in the wholesale rearrangement of goods, the cup somehow has remained with me). This is not all nonsense.

More than once, my mother had raised the question of the deposition of the tall brick duplex. My brother said selling it would be okay with him. Not with me. The first time I went home from Alaska, I took my mother a china teacup painted with forget-me-nots. She kept it on a shelf with a dozen or so other ornate teacups; things I had no desire to own but all the same wished to be there. I have never known whether the forget-me-not is the state flower here because it is abundant or because somebody thought it pretty. Or is it because nobody wants to be forgotten? Despite what the folklore suggests—you come to Alaska to be forgotten, to get a new name, a new Social Security number, a new story—nobody wants to be forgotten in the hearts of those he loves or used to love or wishes he had loved more or better. Even some of those drifting, westering men left a trace of something between fame and notoriety. Even they might have wanted to be remembered.

I thought fixed stars did not burn out. When my father died, it was the end of our family constellation. While my brother remained close at hand (though neither of us could ever be close enough at hand, it seems), I drifted westward until I dropped over the horizon. And I often think I might like to go farther still, to India, to the interior of Africa, places where I expect to see people on the most ragged edge. And more often still, I crave the few remaining open places: Antarctica, Baffinland, and the place Arabs call the Empty Quarter. Places like these scare me, but that may be why it is necessary to seek them out.

And the cat? And my things?

Across town, I have a storage locker. My books live there, my out-of-season camping gear and skis, chairs and stools I have no need of in my cabin but someday might. A friend and I visited this locker to retrieve a mattress when I got my new house. "This place," she declared, "is all about divorce." I think so too, and my prejudices are confirmed in what I see: the seedy haste with which people have come and gone in the battleship-gray halls, along the splintering plywood floors, past door after door after door, several with warnings of foreclosure stapled to them, leaving behind dead flashlight batteries, stray socks, unmatched forks and spoons, tiny Barbie-doll shoes. The cost of a storage locker is the same no matter what it contains.

Today is drippy, dreary. It's the kind of day when you wouldn't be too uncomfortable in a tent. For a while. Until you got tired of reading on your back, your side, your belly, until you got hungry and had to go start the camp stove, until you needed to pee.

Nobody knows where the Magyars came from. Somewhere out of the east, I guess, headed west. They drank blood from veins in their horses' necks as they rode. They burned cities and farms, and scared plain folks so much they called them Hungarians because they reminded everybody of the Huns. And then they got tired of it, I guess. And they settled down, built cities and towns of their own, and lived there.

Falling In

Sooner or later, it happens to everybody. You're out on a river and suddenly you find yourself in a complicated spot. The current has gotten faster, the water deeper, the bottom less certain under your boots. If you look down, you can see water climbing right up your legs while they begin to wobble with the effort of just holding you in place. If you look down long enough, you can make yourself dizzy. Maybe you could have gone back to where you came from. But that's impossible now. Just to get this far, you've stepped crab-wise, meaning to simply go across, but in fact going across and down. It's all upstream from here.

It had been a while since I'd last fallen into a river. Alaska rivers are scary. Glacial rivers run hard and gray, they dare you to try to find out if there's a bottom down there by showing you their braids of silt and gravel not so far from the bank you stand on. I prefer clear water. In Alaska, clear water is always deeper than it looks. There are stories: The guy who fell in while dipnetting and rode on down the river, his muscles all locked up in that icy water. He was lucky; he rode into a back eddy where somebody found him on his hands and knees, too stiff to get himself out. Or the guy who fell off the dock behind the Pump House restaurant and just never came up. Or any number who take tumbles and roll through fast water until they fetch up downstream under willow scrub.

For a long time, I used only hip waders when I fished. A bootful of water at a time, I thought, was enough to hold my attention, to keep me out of trouble. But there are always those spots, those slicks of flat water on the side of a cut bank across a wicked current that no amount of line mending can counteract. Deep holes against rocky bluffs that shade the river the better part of the day. It's in such places the big fish live; it's part of the reason they're so big.

So I look for a good stick to wade with. Sometimes I'll take an old ski pole, but usually I can find a good birch stick left by the beavers. If I'm lucky, it's even gnawed to a point. But there weren't any beaver sticks along this stretch of river. My wife and I were camping in a good spot, and the easy wood had all been gathered up and burned in campfires. So I cut myself a stick out of some alder scrub. It was a lousy stick; I saw as soon as I cut it that it was too short. I like a stick that's at least shoulder high so I can lean into it. And it was skinny and green, too. This stick was going to have to do, though, because I didn't want to ruin another alder bush and because I had gone there to fish, not cut sticks, and it was time to be getting down to it.

I wanted to wade across the back of this pool and try along a steep bank. A bright red king salmon was resting in the pool, but I wasn't interested in him. I was hoping for a rainbow trout and was sure some were hanging around, waiting for eggs. I'd tried the edge of the current on my side of the creek and had turned a trout over, but he was too smart for me. On my next cast, I got a big grayling. That was okay, but I wanted the trout.

My new chest waders were the cheap mail-order kind, but I could roll them up and fit them in my backpack, and if I tore them up crawling through the bushes, I hadn't lost much. But to get them to fit my long legs, I had to accept a size made for somebody twice my girth. It was like wearing a trash bag with legs.

When I came to that tricky spot in the river where I needed two good steps to reach the easier water, I could feel the push of the current, and it said, *too much.* I could feel my flimsy stick vibrating in my hand; maybe it even hummed *woo-woo-woo* in sympathy with the river. Standing midstream clutching my stick in my right hand, my fly rod in my left, Red Sox cap faded to pink on my head, I could see there wasn't a way back.

Still, there are precautions. I've always meant to buy one of those elastic safety belts to go around my waist. But every time I see the price, I flinch. Instead I have sometimes used a bungee cord, or a bright turquoise polyester necktie, or on this day a piece of skinny nylon tent cord.

Up the river, my wife was doing her own thing. Not fishing, though she had a license and a rod, but picking up and examining odd-looking river rocks, watching the swallows fly in and out of the nests they'd made in the far bank, making our camp more of a home with proper places for everything. Together we were imposing our human conditions on a place that could do just fine without our presence. The river was not particularly mindful of my situation. I couldn't stand there all day, so I took the first step of the two I needed.

I wonder about the line between conscious and unconscious acts. I found myself going under maybe a hundred, a hundred fifty feet downriver from where I'd taken my last step. I wasn't thinking about how I got there; I was thinking about not drowning, if I could be said to be thinking at all. While I was going down, I was reaching for the bottom. I wanted air, and I was afraid. If I could just hit bottom and push up. I don't think I ever hit bottom. Instead I gave a couple of hard scissors kicks, the kind they teach you in lifesaving class when it's time to bring the cinder block off the bottom of the pool. I came to the surface with my fly rod still stuck in my hand and my traitorous stick gone down the river forever.

I used to think, or maybe to wish, that life could be seen as a series of doors, doors we would pass through and, in passing, change everything. Some of it is words, or my belief that words make us who we are. So that while I stand in the shallows looking through my fly boxes for something that will work, I am not literally muttering, "Which fly, which fly," like a nattering bag person at a city bus stop, but I am thinking just that idea while all sorts of information pours in from my senses, from my memory until I make my pick. The chartreuse Woolly Bugger it was that hooked me the king salmon I couldn't land but had to try for after watching it swim around all day.

Yet to remember it at all is to put it into words. I recall an image: my wife turned to look over her shoulder. At the sound of the splash? Then she was there above me where I had been washed into a back eddy at the base of a steep rock bluff, taking my rod from me so I could more easily climb up. Then a series of bad choices as I tried to climb and got to a concave part of the rock I couldn't get over. I think I was shaking then; I was alert to the river below me and to how easy it would be to fall in again.

The round hill country around Fairbanks is made of loess, windblown silt. Somewhere down deep in the hillside I live on must be some sort of rocky core the loess fell against day after day for ages, until wind and water and gravity rounded its shape. It's the way words pile up on an event and turn it into what we remember.

That night in the tent, I thought I must have gotten a case of heartburn from our backpack meal. The next day when the weird aching in my ribs wouldn't go away, I figured out I must have busted a couple of them. So then I thought I must have toppled over onto my left side and hit pretty hard. I was starting to find my way through the previous day's event. I was starting to make it into a story.

I want to say how little my life has changed from my dunking. You could say it was almost a drowning. I didn't want to. Slow and clumsy on land, I always thought of myself as sleek and assured in the water. Water knew me for a friend. When I first saw the ocean, when I jumped in and swam down the front of a wave and it dragged me across the sandy bottom and spat me out back into the sea, I laughed. Back on the riverbank, a few gallons of water in each leg of my waders gave me that Popeye the Sailor look. I laughed at that, too.

But this had not been a friendly encounter. Later in the summer, fishing slow water, I stumbled, mired up in a muddy bottom. I felt it in a rush of blood up my neck, a sense my ears were standing wider away from my head than they usually do. Like a dog or cat made alert to a distant noise, but the noise I heard was panic. Was that all? Had I learned to move more gingerly through the world, sticking closer to the shallows, searching for the easier way? Or was it that my self was sneaking up on me and catching me by surprise? I had been scared down to my bones by that ride down the river. If my brain couldn't find the words to tell me, then my muscles and blood would.

How can I tell a story I'm still trying on for size? One day on the river I went under. I went a long way, a hundred feet or more, through sweet clear water and didn't meet a single soul. Came up to find my wife worrying over me. Crawled out and laid myself down on the sunny riverside and raised my legs up to dump the gallons of water turned warm as pee. Bruised but whole, I was alive, alive, alive.

I Built a Little Boat; or,
The Necessity of Failure

If failure is inevitable, why try?

In the tight confines of the basement, I practice some clumsy acrobatics as I maneuver the floppy strakes—sixteen feet long and roughly a quarter inch thick—into the order they must take on their way to becoming a canoe. When I pick up one of the narrow strakes to be positioned at the top of the hull, just below the gunwales, it snaps at the scarf with a crack. To my ears, it resounds like a rifle shot. The epoxy bond has failed, and before I'm done it will have failed or partly failed on three others.

I keep a wooden chair, an old elementary classroom chair, down here. My thinking chair. I sit. I sit like a grasshopper on the little chair, and I think a variety of things: I think, *This expensive kit boat is ruined even as it is scarcely begun.* I think, *The family I'm making this canoe for are Dan, six-three and about 230 pounds; Ingrid, five-two and maybe 110 soaking wet; and their four-year-old daughter, Molly, about 40 pounds and growing.* How could these flimsy strakes bear them up in the water anyway? I ask whether I ought not quit now.

•　•　•

Then I ask, What went wrong? I admit I don't know, but my only solution is to use a Dremel to get as much of the dried epoxy out of the scarfs as I can and try again. Because the one thing I do know is that I won't quit now.

Now's maybe not the best time to admit I was trepidatious about this project from the start. Yes, it is a kit, but just looking at the various unpacked pieces scattered around the floor, the slender and vague instruction booklet, I see it's probably beyond my limited skills. I'm not sure Dan and Ingrid really wanted a boat. It was my idea pressed on them. But this very boat is what the family settled on.

The online promotional information and the color catalog promised a canoe both lovely and functional, a perfect boat for a family of three. On the Web site, a series of dials suggests the boat will be mostly stable—a plus two. And easy—a three out of ten on the difficulty of construction scale with "no tricky joinery." An online photo album offers shots of happy builders paddling their beautiful canoes. By this stage of my life I should know better than to trust the pictures, having been seduced by them again and again as a boy. There on the top of the box, in color, was a perfectly assembled and painted model identical to the one inside the box.

◆ ◆ ◆

Upstairs, I keep another kind of thinking chair. This one is on wheels, which sits behind my small computer desk. I can touch-type, and on a good day, working on the computer can be like playing a musical instrument. I don't need to look at the keys, don't necessarily even need to look at the screen. I can just think into my fingers. Since my brain—anybody's brain—can think faster than I can type, somehow my thoughts must be geared down to my typing speed. On good days, it can work that way, too.

On not-so-good days, I stutter between thought and act. I get snagged on the not-quite-right word, on the poorly cast sentence. Sometimes it's better to go on, keep typing, knowing I will return to what I've written many times to smooth and straighten sentences, knowing that at some unexpected moment the word I need will occur to me. It may arrive at an inconvenient moment, and I may have to work to save it until I find a piece of paper to catch it down on, but with any luck it will come eventually.

• • •

When my brother and I in our haste to dig into our model airplane or car kits tore into the packaging before we could finish the car ride home, our mother warned us we'd lose the pieces, and we often did. She warned us to read the instructions, but we rarely did. So midway through our work we would discover a part was missing, or we'd see a part that needed to go on the inside was many glued steps away from its place.

Though I've unpacked and inventoried parts this time around, I've still not learned. Once again, I am outside my limits and have already screwed things up. Not everything we do is irrevocable, though. Just as I learned that with a knife blade and nail file, glued plastic parts could be broken apart and reassembled with the aid of lots of rubber bands and strategically placed fishing sinkers and cardboard props, I learn that the damaged strakes can be reassembled, too.

With the Dremel, I grind away the misfitted wood and epoxy. I have already begun the long, slow fall from the Platonic ideal of the lapstrake canoe promised in the brochure. I add more epoxy, trying my best to align the strakes correctly again, and put the heaviest weights I can jury-rig on top of the joints. More epoxy, less wood. Epoxy is a miraculous substance. And wood joined by epoxy will splinter and break before the epoxy fails. So maybe having more epoxy in those scarfs is better, huh?

Despite the inconclusive evidence before me, I need to believe that.

It's only on the following morning that I can test the repaired strakes to see if they will hold together. Gingerly, I pick them up nearer the scarf. Yes, they hold, but I feel I am handling something made of glass. That's no way to visualize a boat.

Lapstrake boats have been around a good while, since at least the second century AD. Viking longships were lapstrake designs, and the long strakes are thought to make for a more stable boat. That matters in a canoe, a boat that in my experience is pretty unstable. What I do best in a canoe is flip over.

This canoe is a fake lapstrake. The strakes have been precut with rabbets running along the back of each one so that the strakes will uniformly rest against one another without any careful work with a plane (no tricky joinery!). I still must taper the rabbets so the canoe will come to a point at both ends. That's my next task, one I also do with the Dremel and a sanding drum. Mostly, I am eyeballing each strake, trying to bring them all down to the same degree of taper, but there is no way of knowing.

Actually, that's not true. I could carefully measure and mark off a series of lines along the strakes and, using a caliper, measure each spot down to tiny fractions of an inch. Forget that. I will eyeball these.

◆ ◆ ◆

Artist Sol LeWitt says, "The idea becomes a machine that makes art." When I see this quotation beside a small wooden assemblage, all white, a series of cubic designs with a built-in variation—but nonetheless a systematic variation—I take his point. As the execution of an idea, this construction can be a very nearly perfect art machine, fully imagined and infinitely expandable.

The canoe kit too, any kit really, is a manifestation of the Sol LeWitt ideal: an idea just waiting to be executed, with luck nearly perfectly executed. For LeWitt, the conception is the point. For me, whether it's a boat made of wood or an essay made of words, the execution, the attempt, is what matters the most. A teacup that won't hold tea has failed in its purpose. And an essay?

Here's the thing about writing, whether essays or stories or poems: there is no kit. I'm taking a germ of an idea, kind of like the minute dust particle that helps a snowflake become a snowflake, and build on it. Though what I come up with will in no way resemble the symmetry of a snowflake. And my purpose as I begin is not clear, not even to me—especially not to me.

◆　◆　◆

I fear I have passed from a kind of scientific certainty to a rougher art, from a goal of mathematical precision to a hope for elegant accident. This is a defining moment, both for the boat I am building and for me. I have been here before, and each time I have found myself willing to eyeball rather than measure, to accept a certain amount of risk that comes with the looser (and potentially more inventive) parameters of art. The canoe, though, if it is to be anything at all, must be a sturdy, reliable boat.

Or it won't be. Because here is my real cavil with Sol LeWitt: imperfection, that gesture, that crooked thing, that reality stands between what I can conceive and what I can actually do. Imperfection may be at the heart of every creative (or even semicreative) act I perform.

◆　◆　◆

By now it should be clear that for me this project will not be easy. If it were, it would hold no interest. The ideas I want, that I want to build, are hard ideas, and when I begin I have no idea where they might lead me. I know that the ideas I'm seeking, the ones that have been the germ of an essay, are complicated, beyond my easy reach.

My struggle is not so much about "the perfect being the enemy of the good," a phrase popular with politicians when they vote in favor of a law they don't entirely like. My struggle is about the recognition that imperfection is inevitable and how much effort I will spend doing all I can to keep it to a minimum.

It need not be this way. A person, a Jackson Pollock kind of person, might very well start as far away from Sol LeWitt as can be imagined. In the Hans Namuth film, Pollock seems to attack the pane of glass that stands in for a canvas with no apparent plan or design in his head. He paints, and each gesture leads him to another until finally, in some private, intuitive way, Pollack senses completeness. Whatever he came to do in this particular instance is done. The whole question of imperfection may be set aside.

Regardless of whether I have intended for it to be, this canoe seems to fall somewhere between that Sol LeWitt sculpture, where the idea is cleanly carried out in its execution, and a seat-of-the-pants struggle between me, these slabs of wood, and my few tools.

This is not the first boat I have built. The first was an eighteen-foot sea kayak, also a kit, the *Mighty Snagglepuss*. I made mistakes there, too. If you sight along the starboard side toward the bow, you'll see a slight bulge a foot or so from the tip, the eponymous snaggle.

◆　◆　◆

While conceding my heavy reliance on the Dremel, I want to say I've come to prefer hand tools and the slow work they allow. To that end, I've done some shopping at Liberty Tool, an old three-story general store in Maine, now filled top to bottom with semi-obsolete tools. I've bought three wood rasps, coarse, medium, and fine; a Stanley low angle plane (and had the blade sharpened); and dozens of C-clamps. I've bought a brand-new Japanese-style pull saw. And this major electrical expenditure: an excellent Makita orbital sander.

I have pretty much failed with my efforts to master the plane. I've found ways to fake it by using a coarse sanding drum in a quarter-inch drill. Instead of piling up elegant curls of shavings, I resign myself to grinding the wood down to sawdust.

My pal Kes says it's a shame I've not mastered the plane, a "nearly perfect, simple hand tool." Yes, it is, and yes, he is right. Here may be the place where questions of art and craft come together. There are tools, and how well we work is directly proportional to how well we use our tools. While there may be many for boat builders, there are actually very few for a writer. I work hard to master my writer's tools. I see I'll have to try harder with the plane.

◆ ◆ ◆

Now I have ten long strakes laid out flat on two sawhorses. I drill holes one-sixteenth of an inch in diameter along their edges and insert copper wires. I stitch the strakes together and they come to resemble a multipaneled tablet, a deci-tych if there could be said to be such a thing. When I tighten these wires by twisting them together, they will lace the curved strakes up into a canoe-shaped object.

As I twist the wires tighter, the hull begins to rise off the sawhorses. But it is lopsided and flimsy. By now I've bought a supplementary instruction book, in which I read that wire ties can sometimes be substituted for the copper wires. I rush out and buy some slender wire ties and try to use them to pull the stubborn ends of the boat into the sharp double prows a canoe is supposed to have.

Traditional lapstrake boats don't work this way. Traditional boats have a backbone, a keel running the length of the boat. Traditional boats are formed by using molds. The strakes are built up along the molds, and then the molds are taken away. And in the most traditional of all lapstrake boats, bentwood ribs line the inside of the hull to add stability.

This kit comes with two bulkheads, and I try to use the bulkheads as if they were molds. It doesn't work. The wire ties don't work either. I keep tightening the wires, loosening the wires, pushing and tugging the boat until it begins to look a little more shapely, a little more symmetrical. But I feel I am building an untrustworthy contraption.

I sit in my thinking chair again. I find myself bouncing between a cranky anger, an anger that can provoke something you'd have to call a tantrum, featuring throwing, breakage—damage making things worse. Or a mopey depression where I just sit and stare at my disaster in the making. Neither frame of mind is especially useful.

• • •

When I was invited to talk to a group of beginning writers, I chose for my subject "The Necessity of Failure." And I began with a note I had made for myself in my pocket notebook: "If you aren't failing, you aren't trying hard enough." My audience was uninterested in this idea; they were bored, even angry. One person stamped out. What I intended to say was that good writing comes from risk: jumping off into ideas beyond our vision of their meanings, beyond any clarity about the reason to write them. And sometimes—often—beyond our skills to bring them to some sort of understandable whole.

I have considered whether Pollock freed himself from the nagging question of imperfection. If he were completely free of it, making one painting would have sufficed. There must have been some something in Pollock's head that would insist he make another painting, and then another. Inside is there a Platonic notion, a notion of a fully realized painting that he keeps looking for? Probably not. But how, then, does he know when he's done? Where is that line between "not enough" and "too much"?

• • •

When our family went fishing at Falls Mills Dam when I was a kid, I soon lost interest in watching my bobber for a bite. My brother and I wandered off and explored the boats pulled up on the bank.

Falls Mills was a no-motors-allowed lake, something I grew to appreciate when I became a serious fisherman later. The boats were homemade clumsy builds from whatever wood was available. Swamped and rotting, they still offered an invitation: a boat was a way to travel beyond our landlocked lives, a way to explore a bigger world. Maybe the boat bug bit me then. But how can anybody live near water anywhere without wanting to take to boats?

So when I found myself spending some summer months every year in Maine in a house along Gouldsboro Bay, I knew I must build a boat. And then another. As frustrating as the canoe has been, I doubt it will be my last boat. It contains a wish, an idea. I suppose Sol LeWitt has got this part right: it's the idea of all a boat can be, as much as the fact of the boat before me, that keeps me going.

*　•　◆

To help realign my thinking, I don't ask, *Can I do this?* To do so is to admit to the certainty of failure. Instead, I have to ask, *How can I do this?*

The bulkheads, now wired into the ends of the boat, will be sealed with epoxy. They are not precisely where the instructions suggest they ought to be. They're close as I can force them. In order to cool the strakes behind the bulkheads, I've mixed epoxy with wood fill—very fine sawdust—to the consistency of peanut butter and slathered it into the seams. Because I have a hard time reaching deep into the boat, what results is a mess of droopy, dripping goo. That these sections will be covered over by small decks is no consolation. Eventually hidden from view, they remain an emblem of my boatbuilding at its worst.

Maybe it is time for an existential shrug. It seems to me people use the word *perfect* too freely. Sometimes you just have to live with your weaknesses, the mounting imperfections. Here's a big one: the bulkheads should press against the small decks, making two watertight compartments at either end of the boat. I make a test, taking the decks and simply placing them on the hull, and see there's a three-quarter-inch gap. The bulkheads, both wired and epoxied into place, aren't going anywhere. When winter comes, when I leave off the boatbuilding until the following summer, I will fret and scheme for some way to close that gap without making another epoxy-fueled mess.

Now I must mix some epoxy with silicone fill (to the consistency of salad dressing, the instructions suggest—but would that be oil and vinegar or blue cheese?) and caulk each land where the strakes overlap. I mask each inside and out to try to control the flow of the thickened epoxy and begin. My mixture is closer to creamy Italian.

After a person works with epoxy for a while, he makes some useful discoveries. Epoxy will not bond to number 2 plastic. Or cellophane or waxed paper. Or other forms of plastic such as PVC. One discovers that as messy as it may be to mop up excess epoxy drips and runs, it's much easier and finally neater than allowing it to dry and attacking it with rasps and sanding drums. In this case, cellophane packing tape will do the trick for masking. It's wide enough to allow for some slop.

The kit has come with small syringes for use in squirting the epoxy along the joins. Their volume is way too small, so I've gone to a medical supply store and bought some extra-large syringes used for irrigating wounds. Much better.

I'm caught between two considerations. Above all, the boat must not leak. So the strakes need to be fully filled with epoxy. But the appeal of a lapstrake boat—call it the dock appeal—is in the way the strakes catch the light and shadow. As the epoxy settles into the grooves, it will find a natural level, a level that would be perfectly even if the strakes were running along a clean horizontal line. But they are not.

I begin the tedious job of augmenting fill in some places and rasping it out in others. Dan comes to my rescue by lending me three strange little rasps he bought when he was considering a career as a sculptor. These things are variously shaped in curves and bobs, bristled with steel barbs and knobs that cut through the epoxy at sharp angles and make the strakes stand out as well as I can make them.

◆ ◆ ◆

My work is made of words. Words themselves keep me, must keep every writer, from working like Jackson Pollock. Words come freighted with meaning, and despite the efforts people—think of the Dadaists and Gertrude Stein—have made to tease apart words from their meanings, it seems it can't be done. Or at least I can't do it. I cherish the sound of words, the rhythm of words when jammed together. At my best, I think my words can be built in this musical way—meaning can be enhanced. But at the rock bottom, words have meaning. A kind of Zen koan occurs to me: words get me into problems and words do the best they can to get me out.

As with the boat, it is impossible for me to start from nowhere. Nor can any of us.

◆ ◆ ◆

Hours have passed, and as I am working on the boat only a few hours a day, weeks have passed. I realize a second summer has come and gone. The gunwales are in place and have been rounded off; the strakes are epoxied, and the fiberglass cloth has been laid in the floor of the canoe. But on the underside of the hull, I've let the fiberglass cloth blister under the epoxy—probably because the temperature in the basement was rising as the epoxy outgassed. It's ugly, but I probably can't fix it. *Well*, I tell myself, *it's the bottom of the boat*. Still, it's there. It's there. Get used to it.

I prime the hull.

As we get ready to leave, Mike, our winter house watcher and an excellent carpenter, comes by to check on the house. He looks the boat over. "You're gaining on it," he tells me.

Each time I take off, I find it hard to find my groove again. Granddaughter Molly has come down into the basement and has pronounced the boat "not very decorative." What can I do about that? Maybe paint it yellow.

Finally, I begin a frantic rush just to get the thing done. I put in the seats; I glue down the small decks and simply accept the fact of the bulkhead gaps. At the end of this long day I feel I have done everything poorly. Every cut has been off-kilter. The triangular decks are a little uneven. After I epoxied the pieces of wood for the seats, I noticed a remnant of blue tape under the epoxy. I tried to get it out with one of Dan's special files and probably just gooped up the ridges with epoxy. There is still a remnant of blue tape.

In the morning, it doesn't look so bad. I'm not sure what has changed. The light? The barometric pressure? Sometimes things just happen this way. It has become harder to find that place near one of the bows where the hull seemed to curve inward. I don't think it went away or righted itself when I wasn't looking. It could be that the possibility of the boat's being used begins to overtake the many failures in its making. I have begun to accept what the boat can be. I am gaining on it.

Maybe, I think, *painting was for Jackson Pollock like sex.* Filled with possibility, and so satisfying he wanted to do it again and again.

◆　◆　◆

I consider making little handles by cutting away pieces of the bulk-heads. And I don't feel so bad about this idea when I see finished boats on the Web site with holes drilled through the hull at either end to accommodate rope handles. Those boats would have leaky bulkheads, too, right?

Perhaps my dawdling has had something to do with the last hard task before me. I must varnish the boat. A better-than-average painter, I've not had much luck with varnish. Truly, the boat would be just fine without it; all the wood has been coated with epoxy anyway.

But there are expectations. I sand. And I apply the first coat with a foam brush. In principle, I'm against foam brushes, having learned to paint from professional housepainters who even disdained rollers. My reading tells me foam works better than a bristle brush, and my experience confirms it. The first coat looks pretty good.

Maybe I don't tack between coats carefully enough, because when the second coat dries, I see a twinkling universe of dust particles caught in the varnish. I sit in my thinking chair. Disgusted. I should have known better. I should have taken more time.

For the third (and what for now will be the last) coat of varnish, I tack the boat down twice after sanding with two rounds of damp paper towels, and then two rounds of tack rags soaked with paint thinner. This works. The interior of the boat looks pretty good again. I quit while I'm ahead.

Now, except for the final primer and that yellow top coat on the outside of the hull, the boat is all done. Except it's never really done. I regret that blistered fiberglass. I'm not sure I can keep from trying to fix that before the boat gets away from me. And the better instruction book has made me feel that any fewer than four coats of varnish constitutes a moral failure. In one sense the boat is pretty much done. In another, it never can be.

◆ ◆ ◆

Here is a collision between the intention and the act, that place I always find myself in, the place Sol LeWitt seems not to consider and Jackson Pollock may very well have jumped right over.

There is no way to fix all that is wrong with this boat. There never is. But if the boat is to be a boat and not an awkward impediment in the middle of the basement, it must go into the water.

That's okay. If each painting must be imperfect, through that imperfection art would find a way forward.

One summer shortly after I graduated from college, I stopped by to see my mentor and friend Herb. He was working on a painting, and he kept working as we talked. The radio was tuned to a jazz station. The canvas was a kind of skyscape, clouds painted in one grid laid over another, one of a series of such skyscapes. That he could carry on a conversation, listen to the radio, and paint at the same time can only make sense when I consider how all three fed into the same question: about jazz, Herb said it was all about variation. I think of a good horn player's sixteen-bar solo break in any jazz standard. He played it last night, same chords, same initial melodic line, and here it comes again, that improvisational jump into the possible and the unknown. His solo will pick up where he left off the night before and when he gets done, some ideas, some possibilities will remain for the next night. Something will always be unsatisfactory, always a bit unresolved. And I saw that Herb's painting worked in much the same way. The problems unresolved in one canvas would suggest the questions that would be the starting impulse for the next.

So, too, before the first keystroke comes my intention. And with the first sentence comes a falling away from what I had intended toward what can be done. There will always be more than can be done.

⋅ ⋅ ⋅

When the last coat of paint goes on this coming summer, the boat will be ready to float. Soon enough, it'll be scratched and dinged, its bottom covered with sandy grit. It's a boat; that's what it's for. I'm not like my Native American neighbors who have different words (and sometimes no words) for tools when they're stuck up on the wall, when they cease to be useful and become something else altogether. Having made a couple of boats, I'm more than willing to take some time to look at boats in museums or hung from the rafters in a garage, but a boat is made to be used, used according to the lights of its owners. It's ready to be launched out into the world, beyond my reach, beyond my control, beyond my imagining. That's what it's for.

Kinds of Ambition

1. DO-LESSNESS

As boys, my brother and I could always be found on the cusp of do-lessness. Weren't there groceries to be delivered, shelves to stock, floors to sweep? There was no time to sit on top of the pop cooler and moon out the window at passing cars, passing girls. And my mom, my aunt Rosie, my dad were constantly in motion doing all those things and more: taking and filling orders that came in over the phone, cutting up chickens, cutting pork chops, keeping the books, paying the bills.

Do-less, one of my mom the chief's favorite words. A word with multiple applications in our hometown, from Homer Jennings—a man who'd maintained he'd had a bad back as long as I ever knew him, a man who could be found loafing on the bench in front of the company store, on a bar stool in the Cricket or the Anchor, or standing on the bridge with all the other loafers—to the kids I went to school with who didn't do their lessons, didn't help out with chores at home, and dropped out only to wind up soon enough just like Homer Jennings.

It's true that after Sunday dinner—a sumptuous meal my parents had prepared and set in motion before going to church—they both dozed over the Sunday paper, or in front of the TV no matter how exciting the ball game might be, while my brother and I often raced around outside with our pals.

Objects in motion tend to stay in motion; objects at rest . . . well, there you have it.

What makes a person want to *do*? Here is a baby at a stage when he is trying to roll over by himself. He can get halfway there, but not the rest. Still, he tries and tries again to complete the maneuver. Here is an older child who has rolled over, crawled, and by pulling herself up with the support of the couch or coffee table, begun to walk. Now she walks. One day she will run and jump.

There's something animal in such ambition, to crawl, walk, run, and jump. But where does the ambition come from to add, subtract, multiply, and divide? To do the calculus? To tell our stories using stuffed animals as actors? To find new words for the telling? To what end and at what far-flung end?

Maybe our ambition is like the snow caves mountaineers build as they ascend, holes bored out of the snow to make a livable space. Between ice and rock, there's a limit to how big some snow caves can be, and up to that point, maybe there's only the limit of how much ambition we have as we dig one.

In our household, there were many "if, then," sentences. If you don't do your homework, you can't go outside and play. If you don't get your grades up, you'll have to quit the ball team. If you don't stock those shelves, you can't use the car tonight. But there was one important "when" clause in many sentences: when you go to college . . . Going to college for my brother and me was as certain as gravity. We would go.

After my mom's death, my wife found a checklist she had made for me among her papers. It was a list of tasks written in her Palmer Method penmanship, a list I needed to complete to get ready to go to college. At the bottom, doubly underscored, were the words "Do something."

Getting us into college, dropping us off at the dormitory, helping us carry our things to our rooms, that was as far as my mother's imagination could see us. As far as her ambition could carry us. Now it was up to us. Her ambition would somehow have to become our ambition. Our first charge: not to fail. Check. Then what?

2. A WAY I'LL NEVER BE

One night as I was coming home from an away ball game, riding in the cold school bus with my coat thrown over me for a blanket, it occurred to me that being a professional basketball player would not be much fun. Yes, the seats would be roomier for tall men, the conveyance, whether an airplane or chartered bus or whatever professional ball players rode in, would be warmer. But the ceaseless jouncing through the empty night would be the same. And there would be many more nights.

That was my first intimation that fame might not be all it's cracked up to be. But wasn't desire for some sort of fame what got me riding that cold bus in the first place?

There went my boyhood ideal, Van Gentry, headed for his senior prom: his dad's little gray Chevy washed and waxed, bare wheels painted black, skinny whitewall tires that were just then coming into fashion. Gentry himself, blond hair combed carefully back, white sport coat, shirt open at the collar. On the seat beside him, the corsage for his date.

Just that glimpse confirmed for me the culmination of how I wished to be. The rest was on the basketball court, where he was all confidence and ease, never seeming to thrash or flail or recklessly lose control. He carried that ease with him smooth-talking a girl in the drug store, shooting pool in the pool room where he wasn't even supposed to be. But somehow, his being there made it all okay. His working in our store made me his satellite, hoping that by sticking within his orbit some of his glamour and basketball grace would rub off on me.

There were boys on Gentry's team, on every team I suppose, whose ambition was to make basketball a pathway to at least a localized fame. To walk down the street, to stand on the bridge, or step into the pool room and be somebody. That was all, that was enough for most.

Still, it was a wish that maybe is best when it doesn't come true.

Early in his presidency, Barack Obama was asked by middle schoolers what was different about his life. He said he could no longer walk down a street and just be himself. I had thought of this during the Clinton presidency, how Bill Clinton would never again be able to walk out to his vintage Ford Mustang, hop in, and go for a spin. Being smart, both of these men must have thought through this problem before they ever stood for president, but could either really feel what it would be like to have such an inescapable self thrust upon them?

In a Joyce Carol Oates short story, "Three Girls," the narrator and her friend catch a glimpse of Marilyn Monroe shopping for books in the Strand bookstore. Though each girl has ambitions of her own, the narrator recognizes, "To enter history is to be abducted spiritually, with no way back." This woman, Marilyn Monroe, dead for decades, and in her mid-eighties were she still alive, lives on naked in a *Playboy* centerfold, her skirt blown up by a steam grate in *The Seven Year Itch*, an image, an icon, scarcely a human being at all.

No way back. That's the downside, to have fame hung around your neck. I think of those rendered pathetic or notorious by fame, basketball player Dennis Rodman, Bill Clinton's would-be lover Monica Lewinsky, Unabomber Ted Kaczynski, Wall Street crook Bernie Madoff. Fame, whether a person seeks it or it comes unbidden, has its consequences.

Maybe I should be grateful that all my ball playing, the fouls, the missed shots, the bad passes, came to so little. All that remains is the troublesome truth I have to offer when I'm the tallest person in the room.

And this recognition: that fame, infamy even, comes with work as well. Gentry's grace was hard-earned, shooting at the goal in the alley between his house and the Episcopal church. Pointless, then, to be grateful to have missed out on a fate that was never mine to begin with.

Now I look out the window beyond my computer at the snowy backyard. I am retired, have retired early because I could get away with it and because I wanted to pursue my own writing while, as I told my students and colleagues, I still had most of my marbles. On a given day, I cannot make a single sentence that seems worth reading.

For years I have taught, and made my students' problems—writing and otherwise—my own. When I quit I sat wondering what to do with a file drawer full of student evaluations, pretty good evaluations. A friend said, "You've got to throw all those away. That's not who you are anymore." She was right, and I took her advice. So who am I now?

When I set out to become a writer more than thirty years ago, I'd not thought much about what sort of writer I wanted to be. One of my teachers in graduate school had spent much of his young working life knocking out articles for magazines like *Sunset* and *Arizona Highways* to underwrite his real writing life. Another, fresh off the success of a movie deal and his involvement in writing the screenplay based on his short story, wondered aloud about how he, how we all, might strike it lucky like that again. Some good topical idea, ripped from the headlines as people say, he thought could make a writer set for life.

If we simply wanted to be a writer, this guy told us, we could go down to the used clothing store, buy a tweedy coat, start smoking a pipe, and sit around on a bar stool. (I know, the image has changed, but not the assumptions.) If we wanted to write, we could go back to our digs and write.

I had gone into my graduate studies wanting to be a writer, but now realized I wasn't sure what it was I wanted to write. I believe there are writers who can grab any old idea and make something of it. I believe there are writers who move with ease from idea to idea. Anthony Trollope, it's said, would write the last sentence of one of his doorstops and simply turn to the next blank page and begin again. I am not either one of those kinds of writers.

I used to offer my students the metaphor of Scrooge McDuck's money bin. Imagine that bin as the accumulated literature of all the world's cultures. We in our current moment sit on top of all that writing, and our job is to make a contribution. With all respect to Ezra Pound, making it new is not possible. Making it a little fresher, maybe so.

Is that what I want to do? And what is the correlation between what I want to do and what I can do? When I look inside, I see a guy who's mildly neurotic, sort of smart, possessed of a good memory, nosy, and scatterbrained and lazy. How to make writing out of something like that?

Memory, it turns out, can be a terrible burden. I have a gift for bringing back to mind every failure, embarrassment, and slight from more than sixty years of life. And I have the weight of an obligation—a self-imposed obligation—to remember all I can about Pocahontas, Virginia, the town I grew up in, which is falling back into the earth one person, one building at a time.

My method has evolved into one of slow accretion, a drip, drip, drip like a runny nose or, with luck, something more substantial like a stalagmite. An idea arrives in my head, and if it can survive my skepticism about its worth, a sentence may come along to push it forward, and then grow into a paragraph, maybe two or three paragraphs. And then often, typically, my idea comes to an awkward arrest. Getting stuck, though, is some assurance that the idea might be worth the struggle. Now I have to clip into my bike pedals, clip into my ski bindings, and go looking for what might come next.

Sometimes the next idea is just around the bend. Sometimes it sneaks up and surprises me. Sometimes I have to look and look. And sometimes I put an unfinished piece aside for some long time, weeks, months, even a year or so. I am waiting for what's next to shake loose.

What, though, is enough?

This is a question not of scale but of value. Do I really have anything to contribute to, to refresh as I've suggested, the idea I am gnawing on? Montaigne says he writes to teach himself, and if by some chance it's beneficial to others, so much the better. Sounds vain, but really there is no other way except to bet that my own niggles are something a reader might share. A long shot, but we are all just people. I think of Alice Munro, who looks into the lives of those near at hand with sympathy and a recognition that even the seemingly most ordinary among us live lives of great complexity. Enough to call attention to them and appreciate their fullness and their mystery. These two writers, then, have come to be my models, not grandiloquent, but plainspoken and determined in their desire to see things clearly and set them down on paper.

To write this way, to think this way, requires a certain humility before one's work. Thanks to the miracle of revision, a person can be better and smarter on paper than his real-life, walking-around self. And it seems necessary to believe that this better, smarter self has something to contribute, something worth putting forward for the world to see. There is always the risk of failure, the risk of self-exposure. What matters most is not letting the ego get in the way. What we write is more important than who we are.

By thinking this way, I have tried to dig out a place for my words to enter the world. Admittedly, it is a small space. But within that space are questions that I find I can best wrestle with through words. Friends who fish with me have criticized me for fishing water too closely, working a hole with cast after overlapping cast before reluctantly moving along. I persist just because you never can tell. Some might say the same about my writing life. I go slow; ideas, like casts, have a certain overlap. The questions can be small but are carefully examined. How else to know their value?

I once bet a friend I'd live to be a hundred; we'd indicate the debt to the winner in our wills. When I think of that odd ambition, I tell myself I'm still less than two-thirds there. Plenty of time. It's not the snows of yesteryear so much as the snows of the years to come that worry me. How can I know what I am able to do, to do at all, or do well? How to keep on doing? There is no way to know; there is no choice but to do.

ACKNOWLEDGMENTS

I wish gratefully to acknowledge the following publications where some of these essays initially appeared: "Obituary with Bamboo Fly Rod," *Bamboo Fly Rod Suite: Reflections on Fishing and the Geography of Grace* (Athens: University of Georgia Press, 1999); "I Held Their Coats: A Study of Two Jokes," *Creative Nonfiction* 20 (2003); "Meditation on My Cousin Lou, Dead at Thirty-Three," *North Dakota Quarterly* 59.1 (1991); "Falling In," *Gray's Sporting Journal* 40.1 (2015); "Other People's Pain and My Own," *The Louisville Review* 75 (2014); "Another Kind of Loneliness," "Glamour and Romance," and the initial publication of "Obituary with Bamboo Fly Rod," *Sport Literate* 7.2 (2012), 9.1 (2015), and 2.4 (1998); "Upside-Down with Borges and Bob," *Alaska Passages* (Sasquatch Books, 1996); and "Mont Sainte-Victoire, Approximately" and "Naked to the World," *Under the Sun* 15.1 (2010) and 17.1 (2012). All citations of Homer's *The Iliad* are from the Robert Fitzgerald translation (Anchor Books, 1975).

Special thanks to the Virginia Center for the Creative Arts, where, during my time as artist-in-residence, many of these pieces began to take shape. And to the following friends, who read and encouraged me in preparing these essays for publication: Kes Woodward, Janis Lull, Sherry Simpson, Jennifer Brice, and Dan O'Neill. And thanks to Bill Meiners of *Sport Literate*, a man I've never met, but who has been a supporter of my work for years.

And, of course, loving thanks to my wife and artistic partner, Margot Klass, whose patience, support, and good example I could not do without.